How to
Improve Your Relationships,
Dramatically...

Methods that really work!

How to
Improve Your Relationships, Dramatically...

Methods that really work!

By Frank F. Loomis III, J.D.

Glenn Publishing
San Antonio, Texas

Warning/Disclaimer:

This book is designed to educate and inform based on the author's experiences. It is sold with the understanding that the publisher and author are not rendering professional services or counsel. If professional guidance is needed, a competent professional should be engaged.

Neither the author nor the publisher shall have liability or responsibility to any person for any loss or damage caused or allegedly caused directly or indirectly by information in this book.

Artwork by Bleu Turrell, copyright © 1999
Interior Design by Aeonix Publishing Group

Publisher's Cataloging-in-Publication
(Provided by Quality Books, Inc.)

Loomis, Frank F.
    How to improve your relationships, dramatically
: methods that really work! / by Frank F. Loomis.
-- 1st ed.
    p. cm.
    Includes index.
    LCCN: 99-63105
    ISBN: 0-9672089-0-4

    1. Interpersonal relations.   2. Interpersonal
communication.   3. Self-esteem.   I. Title.

HM132.L66 2000   158.2
                  QBI99-783

For more information contact:
Glenn Publishing, San Antonio, Texas
glennb@flash.net

Printed in the United States of America.
1st Printing 2000

Dedicated to:

*M*y dear friend, Dorothy Powell Michel. Over the years, you kept telling me that I should help others by writing. You planted the seed. Now, here's the flower. I only wish you were here to savor it.

*M*y precious daughter, Melissa. Without your common sense and creativity, this book would be much less than it is. I am in your debt.

Attention

Companies: Do your representatives have to achieve and maintain sound relationships with clients, customers, patients, or other company personnel? If so, this book could help you.

Educational institutions: Do you teach courses that involve communicative or interrelating skills? If so, this book could help you.

Special discounts are available to you for volume purchases of this book.

For information contact:

Special Sales Department, Glenn Publishing
17906 Winter Hill, San Antonio, TX 78258
Phone: (210) 495-2937 • Fax: (210) 495-3073
e-mail: glennb@flash.net

Contents

How to Improve Your Relationships, Dramatically

How can you improve your relationships?

*W*ell, you can do this by using the special techniques explained in this book. When you use them properly, they can change your relationships dramatically for the better and keep them that way. Generally, they are ways of dealing fairly, properly with people important to you.

Their use bolsters the self-esteem of these persons, makes them feel good about themselves. And this in turn makes them feel the same about you.

Thus, you improve your relationships with those people substantially. And, of course, this makes your life more rewarding, fulfilling, and simply happier.

What persons?

To be specific, by persons important to you, I mean (1) those you love, (2) those who are your friends, and (3) those close to you in your business or job. They are the ones that count here.

And no one can dispute the value of having meaningful bonds with such persons. About the only thing to challenge is the how-to-do-it part.

That is what I show you here. I explain and detail these special techniques. The goal is to help you master them or at least substantially improve your use of them.

The gifted few...

Unfortunately, few persons use these tactics to any adequate extent. Those that do are gifted. That is, they instinctively use them without design or plan. Their use is knee-jerk. And it stands to reason that such persons usually fare well in relationships or are advantaged.

The rest...

In contrast, people in the sweeping majority are trudging through their relationships with balls and chains. Their bonds are not what they could be. And, of course, they don't realize how much this burdens them.

Yes, you can learn them...

And if you're one of these disadvantaged persons, this book can help you. You can learn these techniques. You can conquer them.

When you first use them, however, they will seem unnatural and awkward. You will have a this-is-just-not-me feeling. And at times, you could feel that you are a sycophant, someone obsequious and insincere.

But that will not be true. You simply will be someone sincerely trying to treat people properly. And gradually your feeling of being a phony will fade.

This will happen when you start to see striking improvements in your relationships. And such benefits are sure to come if you consistently apply the techniques you learn here.

If you do that and make dogged efforts, you soon will be using these skills as artfully as do those who use them naturally. You will join that talented group.

And believe it or not, you can surpass most members of that fortunate bunch. That is, you can learn to use these methods more effectively than they do.

Why is that so? Well, because when you acquire these skills the hard way, by studying and practicing them, you enhance your chances to excel. You expend that second mile, that second effort that only awareness and desire can engender.

And these extra efforts will etch in your subconscious the significance, the worthiness of your goal. This will fire you up. That's a predicate for excelling.

Sounds great, but...

At this point, however, you might be saying: *"Sure, my relationships aren't perfect, but they're OK with me. So, why should I bother?"*

And if you're reading this introduction in a book store, you could be weighing whether you should return this book to the shelf. You're wondering if you really need what this book teaches.

Well, at first glance, you would think that reasons to improve our abilities to deal with others should be evident. Nevertheless, sometimes to get us in gear, we need to have our noses rubbed in things we already know.

The obvious...

For example, everyone recognizes the worth of having rewarding relationships within the family. Yes, absolutely, we have to get along as best we can with our spouses, children, brothers, sisters, parents, et cetera. Just think of the multitude of serious situations affected by how well we treat and react to each other in familial bonds.

And consider the vital sphere of making a living. How crucial it is to work well with others in this dog-eat-dog ambience, as many see it.

Thus, it goes without saying that any techniques that will help us interrelate better with persons in our families, professions, jobs, et cetera, are indisputably valuable. Who doesn't need them?

And the list goes on as to the value of these skills. They apply to just about any endeavor involving people-contact. We need to know how best to improve our critical ties with people.

Yes, that is what this book is about. But it is true that some things that you will read here are so basic that they are just plain-common sense. And a few are old hat. They've been written and spoken about ad nauseam. And at times you will say, *"I already know that."*

And you will be right. But do we always utilize things that we know? No, of course not. Rather, sometimes we file them in inaccessible pits of the subconscious. Think of the zillions of times each of us has said: "Darn it, I knew that. Why didn't I use it?"

Yes, that's what happens. We can know that something

is good or bad, a yes or a no-no, yet still fail to use that knowledge. It's almost as if we have forgotten it. But, of course, we haven't.

The answer...

So what can be done about this? Well, to help you, this book scrawls boldly some of your "I-know-thats." It does this so pointedly, that in the future, they won't slip by you so easily.

Also, you will find here some true "I-didn't-know-thats." You'll be so impressed with them, you'll say, *"Wow!"* Their significance will almost scream at you. And to some, you'll say, *"Ughhhhhhhhh! I do that all the time!"*

The bottom line...

In sum, chapter by chapter, I put pivotal things on a monstrous-imaginary blackboard for you. They are "dos," "don'ts," and "how-tos" of improving your relationships.

And they are presented to you in an organized, compact manner. They are not jumbled in the random way that most of us have accumulated what we do know about interpersonal skills. No wonder we retain and practice so few of them!

Rather, here, the concise, precise way that these techniques are taught makes them relatively easy to understand and assimilate. And everything comes together, so that you see forests, not just trees.

Furthermore, I won't put you to sleep with a lot of technical mumbo-jumbo. In other words, you won't have to drag yourself through boring stuff. You won't read ramblingly long passages with complex language delving into psyches and motivations of human beings. That stuff fills too many books.

Rather, this one talks to you in plain English about everyday experiences that you can readily identify with. And what is most important, instantly, you'll grasp bottom lines. That is, you'll have little doubt about what you should do and what you should not do in relationships.

So, now you know. That's what's waiting for you here. And it's yours for the effort. It's the means for you to glean awesome rewards in your important relationships. And that means newly born love and respect from the special persons of your world.

That's a promise.

Now, let's get going.

Yes!

Let's get going!

Step One:

Understand and accept the critical factor of self-importance or self-value that is built-in the character of each of us.

"*I'm the most important person in the world.*"

Now, that statement appears overly egocentric, perhaps even egomaniacal. So, the question is, are the people who feel that way in the minority?

No, they're really in the majority. Yes, deep down, most of us feel that way.

And because it has such a distasteful, unattractive aspect, we will not expressly think it or even admit it to ourselves. It's one of those truths that definitely are out there, but we don't think or talk about it.

But we certainly act on it. Everything we do revolves around ourselves. What's best for us, or where are we in this picture? Or putting it in the singular, "What's in it for me?"

Simple events illustrate this trait. They show how potent self-importance is.

For example, when I get that new telephone directory by my front door, what's the first thing I do? I check to see if I'm in it. Is my name spelled correctly?

Or when that picture of me and twenty-five others taken at church is put on the bulletin board in the church-recreation room, what do I do? Do I look to see how the pastor or other members look?

Absolutely not! I first look for me. I want to see *how I look.* Do I look much older? Will people think I'm putting on weight? Do I look fat? How does my hair look? I couldn't care less how other people look.

Thus, in so many matters, I want to know *about me* first. Where did they put what *I wrote?* How does it read? Or when you talked with her, did she ask *about me?* And when Joe called, what did he say *about me?*

The list goes on and on. And most of us are the same way. It's human nature.

And though this trait, in the abstract, sounds horribly selfish and self centered, it's not all that bad. Why not? Because, it's like irrationally disliking skin, something we all have. It's part of everyone. So it's pointless to knock it.

In that vein, we have to accept the self-centeredness of humans. Of course, the degree of it varies in persons. And that can account for differences, good and bad. But for our purposes here, that does not matter.

All that counts is that you understand that each human being has this self-love trait. Perhaps "self-love" is too strong a word for most persons, thank goodness. But it's illustrative. A more accurate term for most would be self-interest or self-importance.

Anyway, this characteristic in everyone is what you must work with in applying methods. That is, you must meet the needs of people to feel good about themselves. But to do that, you first have to accept that those needs exist.

If you don't, you cannot apply techniques properly. Insincerity will taint your efforts. This will cause outright failure or give you marginally effective results.

To succeed with these methods you have to be absolutely convinced of what you have read thus far. If you're not, read no further.

But let's assume the positive. You accept the above. You understand the humanness of self-importance and its role in what you will be trying to do.

So, next, in step two, you will see how this innate-human trait affects relationships.

How to Improve Your Relationships, Dramatically

Step Two:

Understand and accept that how other persons view themselves after contacts with you, is THE BALL GAME! That is the key to the quality of your relationships with them.

*H*ow rewarding your important relationships in life are, depends substantially, on how the persons involved with you think or feel about you. And as strange as it might seem, this does not depend on how they regard you in the usual way of analyzing persons.

For example, a person, internally, usually will not say: *"I like her because, gee, she's intelligent and so much fun."* Or, *"I like her because of the way she looks me in the eye."*

Oh yes, those things do register, but for different reasons. Persons might make those comments about you to other people.

But generally those things don't determine how they

feel about you. What controls that is how they evaluate you subliminally.

This depends on how you make them feel about themselves after contacts with you. It's the key to what you have to do. Your relations with these people must increase or improve their self-importance or self-images.

And therein lies an irony: *Before you can make them like you, you have to make them like themselves.* Or at least you must make them feel better about themselves than they did before their contacts with you.

This also means that no matter how personable you are, they will not like you if you lower their self-esteem. So, it all boils down to whether you make them feel good or bad about themselves.

That's the ball game. To help you win it, as mentioned, I cite many "dos," "don'ts," and "how-tos." I put them in categories of: "make-feel-goods" and "make-feel-bads." And, from a good-English perspective, these terms are anything but correct or artful.

Despite that, I use them prominently in headings of most sections. They serve a critical purpose. They tell you instantly why you should or should not do something.

This instant comprehension justifies their use. So, in pages that follow is a bundle of these "make-feel-goods" and "make-feel-bads."

And looking down from above, I hope Daniel Webster overlooks an even more-grievous breach. From here on, I use these terms as one word without hyphens and quotation marks. Each will have a capital letter at the beginning of "make," "feel," and "good," or "bad." They will appear like this: MakeFeelBad or MakeFeelGood.

So please ignore the awkwardness and impropriety of these non-words. But learn their messages by heart. Then, implement them religiously in your relations with those important-to-you people.

How to Improve Your Relationships, Dramatically

Step Three:

*G*et down, absolutely pat, the MakeFeelGoods on the pages that follow. You want to do them in knee-jerk fashion. Also, memorize the MakeFeelBads. Those are the things you want to purge from your behavior.

How to Improve Your Relationships, Dramatically

Show Interest,

A MakeFeelGood that works magically!

*F*ew things can boost persons' self-esteem more than having other people show interest in them. And that means *genuine* interest.

It doesn't include casual or simply courteous chitchat, like: *"How are things going, Bill?" "How's your little girl, Melissa?"* Those kinds of supposed concern are not enough. They're no more meaningful than that asinine, *"Have a nice day."*

That deduction no doubt falls into one of those, "I know thats." You could say: *"I don't need you to tell me that."*

But really you do. You need points like that chalked on your mental blackboard. But to make that particular "I know that" more acceptable to you, I'll preface it with, "As you know."

So, as you know, that type of supposed interest reeks insincerety. It's meaningless.

Interest can't have a string attached!

Now here's another example of insincere interest:

An old-school chum, Mary, telephones you. You haven't

heard from her for ages. And even before that, you never had had much contact with her.

But anyway, Mary asks you about your work and family. She acts as if this is the purpose of her call, to bring herself up to date about your world.

After a few such boilerplate inquiries, she gets to the point. *"Oh, by the way, I now work for ABC Insurance. I wonder if I can stop over this afternoon and show you my company's new insurance plan. It's a terrific deal for people like you."*

And it's likewise for Mary's paycheck. So, that's the reality, Mary wants something from you — oh, how often this happens to all of us. Yes, that's her motive for showing supposed interest.

But in fact, she doesn't give two hoots about your work or family. She's the type that usually has an ax to grind. She, in effect, tells you, *"I'm interested in you only because I need you."*

Subconsciously, you realize this. It knocks your self-worth for a loop. And, Mary goes to the bottom of your list, maybe even off it.

So, obviously, that kind of phony interest does not pass muster here. An expression of concern that has strings attached, simply does not work. It never makes persons feel good about themselves.

So, you ask what kinds of expressed interest will leave people feeling good about themselves? Try this one:

Let's say, Sue, a true friend, calls you and asks for nothing from you. She is calling only to inquire about your health and your daughter. That's it!

So, her inquiry is a genuine, honest-to-goodness concern about you as a person. Sue wants to know about you.

Subconsciously, she makes you think, *"Hey, maybe I am important, worth something."* You feel good about yourself, who you are.

Thus, Sue raises your self-worth. And how does this make you feel about her? Well, you like her, of course. And you are inclined to overlook outright, or at least minimize, the importance of any negatives she has in character or demeanor.

Yes, showing legitimate, sincere interest in another person puts that person on the path to liking you. It's that simple.

How to become interested

And to acquire genuine interest in a particular person, you need to develop a mental state stemmed in curiosity. You must find things about that person that wake up in you a feeling to want to know more.

But you ask, *"How can I do that with someone who, up to now, has not particularly made me turn on end?"* To say the least, it's no piece of cake.

Well, one way, is to find something that you really like about that person. Everyone has good points. Things are there. But you have to mine for them, ferret them out.

And it's true, with some persons, hopefully few in your life, this seems impossible. They turn you off so readily.

Nevertheless, you just have to discover their pluses. Then dwell on them. The process is difficult, but the game is worth the candle.

One thing that can help you is to develop a general interest in people. That is, determine and analyze differences in personalities and characteristics that exist among the different persons you know. Those differences can spark your interest in each individual.

You "gotta" find something

Now here's an oversimplified, but nonetheless instructive, way to discover an interesting aspect about someone:

John, a young man in his early twenties, doesn't share the musical preferences of his peers. He hates rock music. His loves are Beethoven, Bach, and Mozart. His taste certainly is different.

And why is it? How and why did he develop this apparently rare preference? These queries pique your interest. You want to know more. So, you find out.

You ask him questions about it. You probe. And you do this earnestly. As a result, John responds elatedly to you. He feels honored, flattered. As do most of us, he loves to talk about something close to his heart. He can go on for hours.

Thus, your bona fide interest in this young man makes him feel important, appreciated, and respected. And he likes you for that.

But in trying to do the same with those in your real world, keep in mind another crucial point. The skit that follows illustrates it. The message parallels somewhat the principle in the Mary-example. (Remember her, the lady with an ax to grind?) But it has a slightly different twist.

Shun shallow interest

Larry and Tim are casual friends. At lunch one day, Larry is asking Tim questions about his love life. He asks him how he's getting along with Sarah, his girlfriend. Tim pauses a bit and reflects as follows:

"Does Larry really want to know? Should I tell him that Sarah and I broke up over the weekend over something stupid? Shall I share with him the gruesome details? Well, never before has Larry shown any true interest in me. So why should he now? And the way he's acting, I wonder. Why, he's even looking around while he's talking to me! I think he's just bored and making conversation. I'm not going to tell him a darn thing!"

So, Tim's gut tells him that Larry could not care less. He answers his buddy, *"Nothing's really new, Larry, same old thing."*

Tim's reaction shows how easily people detect barren interest. It can backfire and hurt a relationship.

This happens, because an obvious insincerity exposes the truth. The questioner is being artificial.

But the converse is also true. People readily can sense bona fide interest. Its genuineness permeates demeanor.

That's why it's so critical to find something about a person that lights a spark with you. That way you will project palpable sincerity.

Stick to things you like

Here's an example:

Let's say Diane, your new acquaintance, is a talented

musician. For you, however, music is on a back burner. So, to make yourself interested in Diane's world, you have to look for something else about her.

It should be something that both you and she enjoy or have an interest in. In this vein, you note that she uses computers extensively for organizing her musical endeavors.

And it so happens that computers are your cup of tea. So, there you have it. That subject opens the door to Diane's world of interests. And she welcomes you.

Thus, things work out extraordinarily well. At a picnic, you two talk your heads off about computers.

Your interest in Diane delights her and makes her feel good about herself. She thinks you're super. Thus, you accomplish your goal.

And it is easy for you, because you're using something close to your heart. It's something in which you have intense interest. That's the point.

So, that's the way to show a guileless interest in another. You share with that person a mutual interest. You stay away from things that bore you and stick with matters that fire you up. Yep, this works.

Thus, as far as making Diane's self-worth rise a few notches, you do a bang-up job. And in the process, you ask her all kinds of things, not only about computers, but about all facets of her world. You listen ad nauseam to endless details about things going on in her life.

Reciprocation necessary?

But does Diane ask you anything about your world? Not a question! Poof…! Out goes the air in your balloon of expectations. You're deflated, discouraged.

But should you be? No, because Diane is just like many others. Some fabulously nice people are the same way.

Usually, they're just unmindful. They get wound-up in the delight of persons being interested in them. So much so, they just don't think to ask anything in return.

If they reflect on it, they likely are ashamed. So, don't fret too much when some nice person does not ask in return anything about you. It doesn't mean all that much.

And keep in mind that no matter what keeps persons from overtly showing interest in you, unmindfulness, shyness, or egocentrism, these people will not change. That is, unless they read this book.

So, with the Dianes of the world, you have to bite the bullet. That means that you have to settle simply for improved relationships with these people. And after all, that's the name of the game, your goal.

But despite their failure to outwardly show interest in you, these persons can do other things for you. They can recommend you, share with you, trust you, and generally project their fondness of you. So, indirectly, the Dianes do reciprocate.

Super technique to make "em" love you

Now let's delve into an amazingly simple way to show people how interested you are in them. It works like a charm. You can use it in many situations. It goes like this:

Imagine that you arrive home late one night and find on your answering-machine a message. At first you're perplexed. You can't figure out who the caller is.

He's one of those who drive people nuts by only giving a common-first name. He just says: *"Hi, this is Bill. Remember me? Please give me a call at 499-453-7923."*

You only know ten-thousand Bills. But finally, after studying area codes in the phone book, you figure out that Bill Smith called. He's a friend from Canada that you last saw many moons ago.

So you're going to call him back. But before you do, you sit with pen and paper. You refresh your memory about Bill. *"Let's see what is his wife's name? Oh, yes, it's Mary. How many kids does he have? Four, that's it. And their names are Tom, Billy, Jerry, and Terry."* So, you write down all pertinent information about Bill.

And then when you talk with him later, your questions about his world absolutely captivate him. Bill is so pleased and impressed with you. After all, you are that interested in him to have remembered all those details. He feels good! Of course, you rise several lines on his list.

That marvelously effective way of showing interest can be used in just about any situation where you have notice. That is, you have time to reflect and gather thoughts before you talk to the person.

Besides telephone call-backs and calls you plan to make, you also can prepare for a meeting with someone. It doesn't matter whether that person is friend, business associate, or even your mother.

Yes, even if it's someone as close to you as Mom. It's just as important. Thus, to prepare yourself for a contact with her you could ask yourself: *"Let's see now, what's the name of that book Mom's reading? What's it about? What else should I ask her?"* And so it goes.

So, here's the point: When you know that contact with someone is impending, give it your best shot. Prepare, prepare and prepare. That's a magical tool to demonstrate interest.

Family

Now let's talk about family, parents, brothers, sisters, sons, daughters, et cetera. Meeting the challenge of showing interest in them is not as difficult as with others.

For one thing, you naturally are concerned about their welfare, pursuits, problems, health, and so on. But if you're like most of us, you don't always show or express your interest like you should.

Fight "meism"

So, overtly expressing interest in family is an absolute must. You just have to do it. And in your contacts with family members you have to resist "meism." *It's the let's-talk-about-me syndrome.*

With family members, you have a compulsion to talk about yourself. We all have it. We think they are more interested in us. And they are.

But they also are interested in themselves. They're no different from other people.

So, typically, you overlook this and say something like: *"Hey, Dad, guess what happened to me at work today."* You then spend the entire time talking to him about yourself.

That's what you do, despite that you really should be

asking Dad something about him. *"How's your shoulder, to-day?" "How do you like your new job?" "What's your opinion about the President's tax proposal, Dad?"*

At times, making yourself do this is just plain challenging. Yes, repressing the tendency to talk about yourself is a mountainous task. And as said, it's especially trying when you're with family.

But with sufficient motivation, you can do it. You must focus on their worlds. Forget yours. Practice, practice, and practice talking about their concerns, their interests.

When you do that with family members, you're telling them, *"Hey, I love you. Also, I like, admire, and respect you."* You're giving them healthy views of themselves.

As a result, each subconsciously says, *"Gee, I too, sort of like myself. Just maybe, I really am important in this world."* And for that, you will be rewarded.

But isn't it different with family?

To that you say: *"Hey, wait a minute, if we're talking about family members, I don't have to worry about them loving me. They already do."*

True, but are your bonds with them the best they possibly can be? Probably not. So, you can improve them substantially by using these special skills. By showing family members the kind of concern we're talking about here, you will make your ties with them as staunch as possible.

Thus, *the more interest you show, the more rewarding your bonds will be with them.* They will love you more and like you more.

And, of course, when you show that same kind of hon-est-to-goodness interest in other important people in your life, they too will reciprocate with better feelings toward you.

Try it. You'll see the magic!

Make Someone's Day
A Potent MakeFeelGood!

*B*y that I don't mean what Clint Eastwood in *Dirty Harry* wanted the bad guy to do for him. I mean make someone's day with a sincere compliment.

Typically, here's what can happen:

After telling some nice lady how lovely her hair or dress looks, she gleefully blurts out: *"Oh, you, sweet thing, you've made my day."* Yes, we're all familiar with that type of delightful reaction.

But we're not familiar enough! Simply because we just don't compliment as much as we should.

And it's such an easy way to make someone feel good. So why don't we do it more often? What holds us back?

Well, answers do exist. And if you learn about some of them, hopefully, this will help you quell the reluctance that plagues most of us. It hampers relationships.

Envy

Some people don't compliment because they're envious. Jim doesn't tell Bruce what a nice looking suit he's wearing. His own suit is nowhere near as attractive or stylish. And by not complimenting Bruce, Jim thinks he's de-emphasizing Bruce's suit.

On the other hand, if he says something nice about it, he's giving it even more attention. And that's the last thing he wants.

Of course, Jim's thinking does not make much sense. But that's what emotion can do to a person.

Jealousy

Another emotion that keeps people from complimenting is jealousy. Because it's more intense, it can be more harmful than envy. Here's a typical situation that many of us encounter:

The Joneses have just purchased a new living room-suite of furniture. It's expensive, beautiful, and matches the decor of their home extraordinarily.

Objectively, someone could go and on about how outstanding the furniture is. But that person is not Beth, the Joneses' "good" friend.

After barely a glimpse at the new suite, Beth says: *"Gee, new furniture. How nice."* That's it. That's all she says about it.

Then, wham, she changes the subject. So, it's obvious that Beth is livid green with jealousy. She makes this so apparent that she miffs the Joneses. They'd like to tell her to get lost.

Low self-esteem

Another reason some people don't compliment is that their self-esteem is at a low ebb. That is, they fail to express admiration because to do so lowers their opinions of themselves.

The patterns that follow are typical:

Joe is a public relations writer for a school. The institution has been initiating a new learning project that has triggered opposition in the newspaper. In his press releases, thus far, Joe has failed to rebut this adequately.

But Alice, a disinterested observer, does just that. In an article that she writes and sends the newspaper, she cogently defends the school's project. Her piece is well written, organized, and most important, convincing. The paper publishes it.

So, Joe writes Alice. He thanks her for the article. But conspicuously, nary a word does he pen about what an outstanding writer she is.

Now what does this omission say? First of all, it says that Joe knows that Alice did what he could not. It also says that he knows that she's a better writer than he.

Moreover, a compliment would be admitting exactly that. And his opinion of himself as a writer would suffer. So, that's Joe's rationalization for not complimenting Alice. His low self-esteem is the key.

Bruised egos

Now, here's another. It's somewhat different but still involves an ego-problem:

Pierre is a person of French descent, born in America. His parents were raised in France. Though they now live in Maine, they don't speak English.

When Pierre was a child, naturally, only French was spoken in his home. Thus, it's Pierre's first language. And, of course, he later learned English in school. So he's fluent in both languages.

Anyway, Pierre and David, a Californian, become internet buddies. By email, they write each other regularly in French.

Ten years ago, David took up French as a hobby. He took a few classes, but mostly learned the language by reading, listening to cassettes, and devoting hours and hours in study.

In that brief time, David has achieved a remarkable degree of fluency in French for someone with no such roots. With amazing clarity, he writes beautifully and correctly in the language.

Well, by now, no doubt you have guessed the scenario. In his letters to David, Pierre never compliments him on his French. Not a word does he say about it. He does, however, commend David about other things.

Does this mean that he doesn't admire David's French? No. It only means that Pierre's ego is bruised by David's proficiency. *"Here I've been raised with French, and this guy can write it better, express it better, and even use better grammar than I. That bugs me."*

So that's Pierre's thinking. And that's why David gets no compliments from him.

Now here's a final pattern:

Bob has just bought a brand-spanking-new Mustang convertible. He can hardly wait for his buddy, Tom, to see it this afternoon. So to knock Tom in the kisser with the car, Bob parks it right in front of his house.

Tom shows up and gives the Mustang a cursory glance. He then says to Bob: *"Hmm! Nice, but I like Dodges. They're a better deal. That's what I am going to buy. I think they're the best looking convertibles on the road."* And dogmatically he adds, *"They're better built!"*

So, as you've no doubt concluded, Tom's the type that can always buy better and smarter than you. He's an I-can-do-anything-better-than-you-can or whatever-you've-got-I've-got-better guy. And usually this type also bitingly tells you: *"Oh, by the way, you paid way too much!"*

That last one is a killer! Nothing can make you feel worse than hearing that, just after you've bought something. But it happens and happens, because out there are zillions of "Toms."

Examples could go on. You probably could add a few. But by now, no doubt you see their common thread, a self-worth problem.

By complimenting you, or commenting positively on your possession, talent, or something you have done, in such persons' minds they put themselves down. Compliments remind them that they don't have what you have or haven't done what you have. That bothers them.

Facts don't change

But these people are deluding themselves. They believe that by giving short shrift to, depreciating, or ignoring good things, they strip them of impact, reality.

That is, Jim puts Bruce's old suit back on him. Beth takes away the Joneses' new furniture. Alice's writing does not outshine Joe's. As it should be, Pierre's French is better than David's. And Bob doesn't have a snazzy Mustang that shows-up Tom's jalopy.

Such are the irrational motivations of persons who fail to compliment because of their inability to accept reality. What reality? Well, the fact that they and everyone at some time will be surpassed in achievement, talent, or possession. So be it!

Those who don't notice

Some don't compliment when they should because they don't always notice things. For example, there's the husband who doesn't note his wife's pretty-new haircut. How disappointing! *"Maybe, he doesn't like it,"* she thinks.

Not true! He's just not being alert!

But he is being just like a lot of us, including this writer. We need to work on this problem.

The remedy: You constantly have to be alert for new things regarding persons important to you. *That is, you must notice their new clothes, hair styles, new things that they have done ("You put up some new pictures!"),* et cetera. Then, you must tell them how much you like those things.

So, be observant!

An understandable reason

Now the above patterns show unacceptable, even zany reasons why persons don't compliment. But some people don't do it for a far more respectable, understandable reason. They're just plain shy.

Yes, many persons are that way. They're not jealous, envious, or worried about their self-esteem. And they do notice good things. But they just have a hard time getting themselves to compliment.

Anyway, if for any reason you don't do it like you should, you're missing the boat to enrich your relationships. So, fight, overcome whatever holds you back and just do it!

If you like something, say so!

Yes, do it! Make someone's day. And watch the magic of a face lighting up. See that ear-to-ear grin. Disarm even an ornery person with a timely, sincere compliment.

And add spice to your words with details. This adds believability and earnestness.

For example, if you like your neighbor's new car, tell her why you like it. That is, detail your likes. The color is a knockout, or you marvel at the quality of the interior, et cetera. This way your neighbor will believe you and not think you're just buttering her up.

And remember, compliments can be about things incredibly simple, like an infectious smile. Tell her or him! Why not? What can you lose?

Nothing! And as I say, and will say over and over here, when you tell people nice things about them, you give them a compelling reason to like you.

You're making them feel good. *So teach yourself, discipline yourself, to give sincere compliments regularly.*

Put this awesome tool to work for you.

Listen Well!
Respond Well!
Two Critical MakeFeelGoods!

*T*hese MakeFeelGoods are offshoots of the *Show Interest* segment. After all, few, if any, better ways exist to show interest in people than to listen and respond well to what they say. Being skillful in doing this merits ample attention here.

This is because using these skills properly, ***shows persons that you think they're important;*** that you appreciate and respect them. And it shows them that you value their observations and opinions. What they have to say matters.

And you go a long way in accomplishing such things when you merely listen carefully to persons' words. If you don't do this, and sometimes regard important-to-you people as babbling children, well, few things can maim their self-worth more.

As appalling as that sounds, many persons do just that too often. They are so caught up in things they want to say next, that they don't care what other persons are saying. The mind-set is, *"Hurry up, finish, because I have something really important to say. And what you're saying isn't worth a hill of beans."*

Sometimes it's disastrous!

Aside from how harmful such behavior is to bonds between people, it can be costly in another way. You can miss something crucial that a person is saying.

Oh, how often that happens to everyone! You don't pay close attention to directions and get lost. Or you fail to listen carefully and don't catch crucial words. Here's an example of what can happen:

Betty and Lisa are close friends. In a chitchat, the subject of crooked, dishonest people comes up. Betty happens to mention Bill, another friend, who works at a bank. She says, *"Bill's not that way."*

Now, Betty tends to mumble. And Lisa is engrossed in what she wants to tell Betty next. So, she doesn't catch the word, "not." Only the words "crooked" and "dishonest" ring in her subconscious. *"So, Bill's dishonest, a trickster,"* she inwardly concludes.

Lisa then sets her goof in concrete. She fails to respond to Betty's comment. That is, she doesn't ask Betty to support the statement. In other words, why does Betty think Bill's dishonest? So, if Lisa were to respond logically and attentively like that, she'd catch her listening-blunder. But she doesn't.

Thus, Lisa commits two breaches. She does not listen well, and then fails to respond.

As a result, the next day Lisa wreaks a horrendous injustice. At a cocktail party, she imbibes a bit too much. In a conversation with her friend, Leona, an official with Bill's bank, the subject of Bill comes up casually.

Because of the drinks, Lisa lacks her usual sense of restraint. She tells Leona what she had heard about Bill. But more correctly, she tells Leona what she thinks she had heard. A month later, without explanation, Leona's bank discharges Bill.

Hopefully, that skit shows how critical sound listening and responding skills can be. And for our purposes, such talents can be enormous factors in how well close relationships fare.

So, with that in mind, some pointers follow. You should try to etch them in your subconscious. And if you follow them, you will make a considerable headway in becoming a good listener and making appropriate responses.

So here they are, a bundle of absolutely *critical "dos" and "don'ts"* of good listening and responding:

Make unwavering eye contact. Yes, this is essential! It makes speakers feel so important.

Lean forward a bit toward speakers. You don't want to miss a single word. That's how intensely interested you are.

Nod in agreement with things you like or agree with. This also says you understand what's being said.

Occasionally, make appropriate-supportive gestures. For example, smile when speakers tell you things fortunate for them. This shows that you like what you're hearing. You share their happiness.

Conversely, wince or frown to show compassion about unfortunate things. In such ways, you buoy persons' spirits with knowledge that someone is on their team, supporting them and sharing good and bad with them. And the amazing thing is that it's so easy. You don't have to say a word. A smile, a circled-index finger and thumb, or a wince can say volumes.

Give undivided attention: Don't be the person who, while supposedly listening, scans a newspaper or glues eyes on a TV. Nor should you be the type who lets a child interrupt a talker and proceeds to converse with the youngster. *"Sorry, Talker, but you take second fiddle to Junior."*

Or during the talker's comments, you don't turn on the garbage disposal. And, of course, you never walk out of the room while someone's talking and later say: *"Oh, I thought you had finished."* The offended talker will want to scream: *"If you had been listening, you would have known I wasn't done."*

Such an unfocused listener embitters a speaker. It's like saying, *"I don't want to listen to you. I could not care less what you say."*

And what do such things do to a relationship? Well, as you can imagine, they're bummers.

Be patient! Hear speakers out. Don't cut them short.

Don't show disapproval! If you disagree with something that's being proposed or argued, try not to show this with a negative demeanor while the person is talking. For example, don't scowl, frown, or roll your eyes. Nor should you use negative-body language like crossing your arms or leaning away from the speaker.

Rather, if you want to express disapproval, you do it verbally after the person finishes talking. But before then, you offer no clue that you disagree.

Don't look at your watch: Never, never do this while the other person is speaking. This says things like, *"Hurry up, will you!" "You're putting me to sleep." "Get it over with, right now." "You're wasting my time."* Needless to say, those implications gall.

Interject: If befitting, and not too disruptive, timely interject an appropriate-terse comment like: *"Oh, yes!"* or *"Right you are."* Such interjections show that you're paying full attention, and that the speaker's words are hitting home.

But let's say the shoe is on the other foot. Yes, you're the speaker, and the listener interjects: *"That happened to me too!"* Don't ignore it like so many speakers do, especially when it supports you like that. Briefly respond by saying something like: *"Hey, no kidding! When I'm through, I want to hear about that. But right now, as I was saying…"*

Respond: When a speaker finishes, be responsive. Some million-dollar-a-year-or-plus-television interviewers often don't do this. They ask difficult, touchy questions. And unless the speakers give provocative answers that invite follow-up, the interviewers act as if nothing has been said. They go right on to the next question. It's like they're not interested in answers, only questions.

Arguably, this is discourteous. A simple "thank you," isn't asking too much. Evidently, the interviewers think that showing such respect would make them appear partial to speakers.

Silence is not always golden: In the worlds of most people, courtesy almost always demands response. Not saying anything can give too many negative impressions like:

- You didn't listen;
- You don't respect the speaker;
- You disapprove of what was said; or
- You think what was said is unworthy of response.

So, don't run the chance of giving someone any such negative impression. Respond!

And this means that you should do so to all communications, written as well as oral. Letters and notes are much easier to give short shrift, because their writers are not confronting you, reminding you to respond.

Now this seems so basic, but *promptly answer those letters and notes!* Not much can be more detrimental to a budding or existing relationship, than to not respond with reasonable timeliness to letters and notes. If circumstances don't permit a thorough reply, at least acknowledge receipt. Promise a further reply as soon as practical. And keep your word.

But within a reasonable time, if you don't send some type of reply, arguably, you're in essence telling the writer, *"Hey, you're not important to me. What you say doesn't mean beans; you don't count."* And you could be sending that message to your mother, father, sister, brother, close or romantic friend, or business associate. Talk about a MakeFeelBad, wow, that's one for sure.

But if you're not one of those (you do reply promptly), let's hope you're not one of these: Many persons forget or set aside in their minds many things writers touch upon. In other words, their replies do not respond adequately to the original writers' questions or subjects. They ignore some and reply only with what they want to say. And too often that only is about their worlds and interests.

So, as to subjects to cover, discipline yourself. When answering that email, letter, or note, put it right in front of your kisser. And before you start to write about your interests, make sure you respond to each matter the writer discussed.

And to motivate you, imagine how you feel when you make an interesting point in a written communication, and it's ignored. So, don't do that to the other person.

Thus, the main thing here is that you must respond to what other people say, whether oral or written. And do so timely. Moreover, do it, even if you disagree strongly with what was said by the other person. At least say something like: *"I appreciate hearing what you have to say,"* or *"That's certainly one way of looking at it."* Such words are not agreement. But they are respectful and courteous.

If the person has made a good point, say so. Even if you dispute it, still say up front something like this: *"You state your point well, Deborah. But did you ever consider…?"*

This way, though you differ with her, you still demonstrate respect for her. That's a MakeFeelGood.

"I know," usually is a poor response. In essence, you tell the speaker, *"You are bothering me with something that I already know about."* Add to that, it makes you sound like a know-it-all.

So don't use *"I know."* That is, unless it really is pertinent that the speaker know that you're already aware of the matter.

For example, you can comment incidentally like, *"Oh*

yes, I know, I heard it at work yesterday." In this context, you're not rebuking the speaker, nor being a know-it-all.

But when it's not necessary to let the speaker know about your prior knowledge, try this: Instead of saying *"I know,"* respond with a *"Yes," "Exactly," "Absolutely,"* or *"Isn't that something."* Here's an example:

Myra: *"Yesterday, Bill got that job with ABC."*

Tina: *"Yes!"* [or, *"Isn't that something."*]

Here's another:

Leslie: *"It's always best to use form 1040 when you have deductions."*

Rachael: *"Absolutely!"*

One more:

Sarah: *"I think Tim did his best."*

Zachary: *"Exactly!"*

Now to drive this point home further, substitute "I know" for the above-emphasized responses. What a difference! Right?

So, strike "I know" from your vernacular.

"I wouldn't know," "I don't know" or *"I don't know that,"* are usually no-nos in the following context:

Maryanne: *"When I was at school yesterday, one of the clerks in the office said that we got a high rating last month in phonics."*

Bill: *"I wouldn't know."*

By responding that way, Bill, by implication, is calling into question Maryanne's capacity to report information, and perhaps even her credibility or judgment. In one sense, it's almost as bad as saying, *"Because I didn't hear that myself, and because it's you who is saying it, I can't believe it. Just because you say something happened, doesn't make it so."*

Wow! That's a bummer! And it sure doesn't do much for Maryanne's self-esteem. Think how much better it would be for their relationship if Bill instead were to say, *"Really, how about that."* What possibly could be the harm in saying that even if he really does have doubt?

Two common no-no responses: The first is almost epidemic:

Alice: *"When I was in my first year at the University, I lived in a dormitory where the juniors and seniors hazed me."*

Tony: *"When I was there, I lived in a frat house. Hey, let me tell you about what we did at a party there one night…"*

The second is a bit worse:

William: *"I just bought a brand-new Mercury. I'm so excited!"*

Silvia: *"Well, Sam and I just got a new Buick. We think it's a knockout. Let me tell you about some of the bells and whistles it has. There's this gadget that…"*

Tony and Silvia's responses are classic, *"how-not-to-do-its."* So, let's rewrite their scripts. Here are better ways to reply:

Before switching the focus to their worlds, they should respond fully to Alice and William's words. That means they should comment and ask questions.

Tony should talk about the hazing Alice received. And

in the process he should ask for more details.

And Silvia should talk about William's new Mercury. She should ask him: What color is it? Where did he buy it? What model is it?

In sum, too many listeners act like they're uninterested in what speakers say. They're waiting only to hear themselves talk about their own worlds and interests. It seems to be the well-trampled path of *"I don't want to hear about you, that's boring. I want to hear about myself."* Of course, this is a turnoff, a MakeFeelBad.

Super way to respond: After the person has finished, try to sum up what you think you heard. Say something like: *"I want to make sure I understand you. Are you telling me that you like this plan?"*

This tells the speaker that you are interested in what was said. You paid close enough attention to get the point.

Moreover, using this tactic regularly, forces you to listen well. You don't want to embarrass yourself by misstating what the other person said.

Answer the questions: Listening skills are also involved in answering questions. To answer a query, you have to understand it. And you won't if you don't listen carefully. And that in turn causes you to answer inadequately.

So, for that reason, many times, people don't really answer questions asked. They give off-point responses.

Thus, questioners have to ask again or give up. This is another example of sloppy, inattentive listening that can affect relationships negatively.

So, listen carefully to questions and discipline yourself to understand them. That way you have the best chance of being responsive. That's part of good listening.

"I hope so." You hear this reply often in TV interviews. Usually, it's inconsequential. But it can be annoying. It goes something like this:

Patient: *"Doctor, do you think this medicine will work?"*

Doctor: *"I hope so. If it doesn't, I'll try something else."*

Obviously, that reply doesn't answer the question. Though this seems minor, it demonstrates the point that: If it's a fair question, you should make sure you really do answer it.

You can assure this by internally asking yourself in a light-second instant, *"Will my intended reply really answer this query?"* If your answer is yes, you go ahead.

So, always try hard to truly answer questions asked. This shows respect for the other party. And it shows that you're paying attention, and you feel the question deserves an answer.

Accomplishing such things just has to be a plus.

When the question is intelligent, say so! *"Melissa, that's a darn good question. I would say..."*

The answer, "Of course," usually is not advisable. *"Were you born in the United States?" "Of course, I was."*

That answer berates the questioner for asking. In essence, it's saying: *"What a dumb thing to ask; you ought to know better."* So, seldom is that response appropriate.

An exception could be when a "yes" or an "oh" precedes it to express emphasis. *"Do you like my dress?" "Yes, of course, it's a knockout!"*

Don't evade questions: Some persons dodge questions.

They listen and understand them but then try to evade them. For example, instead of answering, they defiantly challenge the inquiry. Here's one way they do it:

Question: *"Did John call you?"* Response: *"Why do you want to know?"*

So, why do people duck questions? Usually, it's because they just don't like the potential consequences of the answers they would have to give. Children are particularly prone to do this to avoid accountability.

So you ask, what is the most common tactic used to dodge queries? Well, most culprits beg the question. That is, they give responses that really don't answer the questions asked.

What they do, is employ a fiction. They pretend that the questions are different, more to their liking. Then, they answer the imagined questions.

In doing that, they scorn questioners. And in a sense they deride their intelligence. In effect, the evader says, *"Hey, I think you're dumb enough that I can slip this by you."* It's not only a demeaning tactic, but a deceitful one as well.

But what do you do if you have a legitimate reason for not wanting to answer? Well, be up front with the questioner. But that doesn't mean you have to be discourteous or abrasive, like some people are.

We see their kind regularly on TV. Usually, they're celebrities and public figures, who should know better. They imperiously ignore questions. Or they say, *"I'm not answering any questions,"* or brusquely blurt out: *"No comment."*

In contrast, it can be done courteously so that no one takes offense. This is especially important when the questioner is someone close to you.

Here are ways to do it:

- *"Please forgive me, Jean, but I'm just not able to say anything at this moment."*

- *"Gee, Bob, I'm so sorry. I wish I could answer you, but right now I can't."*

- *"I do hope you understand, Pete, but I can't answer that now. But perhaps, shortly I will be able to help you. I sure hope so."*

- *"Gee, Ashley, right now my hands are tied. But I certainly appreciate your concern. Thanks for asking. I'll get back to you on this as soon as I can."*

As you can see, those responses are empty. But they don't offend a questioner. This earns you respect.

What should you do if the question is a delicate opinion-inquiry? Suppose it's something like: "Do think the president is doing a good job?" Your answer could please or displease.

So try this: Before you answer, probe for the questioner's opinion. If you can't directly ask for it, try to get at least a hint. With luck you and the questioner agree (you have a 50-50 chance). Then, you answer.

But suppose you find out that you two are at swords' points on the matter, what then? Well, you weigh the risk of expressing your opinion. It's touchy. But at least you make an informed decision. You are not walking into a booby trap. That's the point.

Don't delay answering: When you respond to a question, if possible, right off the bat answer it. Don't first add other comments that only tangentially relate to the query.

That's another scenario we see often on TV. A star will be asked something like:

Reporter: *"Did you go to Europe last year?"*

Star: *"Well, let me tell you this, two years ago, I thought I wanted to go there, but I never did. But last year I thought that finally I would go.... [Blah, blah, blah, et cetera]. So, yes, I did go to Europe last year."*

That scenario is somewhat like the old saying: "If you ask the time, you first have to hear how the watch is made."

And it's another example of a listener not giving a speaker's words proper due. A "yes" should be given up front and not at the end of a discourse.

Why do people do this? Usually, it's a matter of ego. They want to put themselves more in the limelight, by saying more than asked. A simple "yes" or "no" doesn't render sufficient attention. It doesn't satisfy ego.

So, use this cardinal rule: If practical, answer the question first, then add other details as appropriate.

Bottom line: Learn and practice proper listening and responding habits. They are skills that can make a marked difference in how well you get along with those persons important to you.

They're definite MakeFeelGoods.

The Interruption,
A flagrant MakeFeelBad!

Don't interrupt!: Unnecessarily interrupting is one of the most galling things that people can do when they're supposed to be listening. About the only breaches of sound interrelating that are as rude or crass as interruptions are some mentioned in the *Listen Well* section.

In contrast to them, the interrupters' abuses are inflicted somewhat differently. These persons let you start to talk but then won't let you continue. Whether it stems from their impatience, ignorance, their egos not wanting you to have the floor, or whatever, they stop your flow. They disrupt.

The mind readers

Most times, they're attempting to read your mind. Or in reality, they're guessing what you're going to say. Their ostensible justification is that your intended words or ideas are useless, no good, or won't work.

A typical such interrupter's thinking is *"I'm saving us both time in stopping you. I don't have to listen to you, and you don't have to say it. So, why don't you just forget it?"*

Many times the guess about what you are going to say

is off target. You intend to say something else. But it's too late, the harm is done. The break-in can brutalize not only your thought, but your self-worth. And unless it's critically important, you do the interrupter's bidding. You stop and clam up.

So that can be the dire result of that kind of break-in. Your inner-self says: *"This person doesn't think that what I say is important or worth a hoot. I guess it isn't. Maybe I'm just not worth listening to."*

That's what can happen to a victim. The interrupter's boorish conduct can take that kind of toll.

Why?

And since such behavior is so blatantly wrong, why in the world do people do it? Well, as mentioned, *impatience is one reason.* They are unwilling to spend the time or afford the talker the courtesy of listening. They don't want to be bothered.

This mental state reeks of disrespect for speakers. And that's exactly the message they get. It can devastate relationships.

But sometimes mind-reader disrupters are just plain *know-it-alls.* They think they actually know everything you're going to say. In essence, when they interrupt you, they're saying, *"You can't tell me anything I don't already know. So, drop it."*

Wow! As asinine as that sounds, some people do think that way.

Thus, obviously, interrupters who think they can read minds are dillies. But others equally harmful also exist.

The others

One group that particularly sticks in the bark is that bunch who commit the cardinal sins of good listening mentioned above. Remember these people? They're the characters who, while someone is talking, look at magazines, glance back and forth from TV, turn on can openers, or walk away from and turn their backs on speakers. Such antics interrupt just as effectively as words.

Thus, those jerks really belong to two flocks: (1) the lousy listeners, and (2) the ill-mannered interrupters. They're both tacky.

The butt in type

To that second-nasty group, add the type person who butts in on a conversation. When an adult does this, blame two or more persons: (1) the one who breaks in, and (2) those who permit it.

The attention seeking child

Often these "butt-inners" are children. For this, we should denounce only the adults. By permitting this, adults are committing two wrongs. They are offending speakers and neglecting their duties to teach children proper manners.

Here's a typical situation: You're telling Bill, your neighbor, about a perplexing-neighborhood problem. Your time is limited. But you need Bill's understanding and help. It is critical.

While you're talking, Teddy, Bill's ten-year-old, breaks in. He starts to tell his dad about something going on at school. Bill and Teddy then enter a lengthy colloquy about the project. They ignore your presence. You want to walk away. But you patiently endure the transgression until it finally ends almost five minutes later.

So why do some parents commit such breaches of courtesy? Why don't they tell their children to butt out?

Well, in Bill's case, he's probably a proud dad showing off his son. Bill's trying to impress you. And in doing that, he's missing an opportunity to teach Teddy some manners. And to you, he's being inconsiderate and discourteous.

The thieves

Yes, Bill's conduct is indefensible. And so is that of line stealers, the thieves. *"Good heavens, tell me about them,"* you say. Well, here are two illustrations:

Thief one, Richard: He and Sheila, husband and wife, are dining with friends, Melissa and Brian. The couples are exchanging tidbits about their recent doings. When Sheila gets a chance to talk, she starts to tell a thoroughly funny thing that happened to Richard and her when they were on vacation.

Before she can get out her second sentence, Richard breaks in. He then tells the story.

He has a habit of doing this. Sheila is creative. She gets an idea to say something entertaining or interesting. She starts to express it. Richard will preempt her, steal her lines, and take over the telling. This happens regularly.

This is because Richard seldom has anything original to say. He's neither innovative nor resourceful. So, as he sees it, to be an interesting conversationalist, he just has to have material. And Sheila has a wifely duty to furnish it.

Supposedly, that's not stealing her thunder. *"I'm just*

exercising my espousal right," he thinks. Sure, sure, Richard, but in the process you're a gross interrupter.

And this particular time you are humiliating your wife. You're in essence saying: *"Hey, Sheila, let me tell this story, because you're going to blow it. Yes, Melissa and Brian, Sheila doesn't explain things very well."*

Thief two, Barbara: She and Jane are chatting. Jane tells her about a new medication to prevent breast cancer that she heard about on TV that morning. Jane follows with: *"I think that soon…"* Barbara cuts her off and takes off on the subject. At length, she expresses her thoughts and opinions about the matter. Jane is left with her tongue hanging out, so to speak.

So, Barbara, in essence, is saying to Jane: *"Boy, that's a darn good topic. Why don't you shut up? I'm taking over. I can do a much better job on this than you."* That's her mind-set that supposedly justifies her larceny.

Some people do this regularly. They delude themselves that the persons from whom they plagiarize topics and ideas will overlook their crime. The stealers think that they are judged only by what they say and not by what they do. Of course, that's fantasy. Logically, people do not tolerate well expressions that evolve from thoughts stolen from them.

Thus, in Barbara and Jane's exchange, Barbara ends up doing all the talking. But no one is really listening. Jane is still there but now no longer perceives anything. That's because she's so preoccupied in her ire. She is seething! And you can imagine what she now thinks of Barbara.

So, it's fairly obvious that line stealing raises Cain with relationships.

Question: Is there anything you can do when you're interrupted? With a child, yes, you can do something. Unless it's urgent, as suggested in the example of Bill, you should tell the child to wait. This is good training for a youngster.

But with adults, it's not so easy. If practical, depending on circumstances, you can ask the interrupter, as delicately as possible, *"May I finish, please?"*

That tactic won't work, however, if you're an attorney doing battle in the courtroom. The other side often interrupts you. It's an attack-mechanism to derail and upset you. That's the point of this mention. An interruption can devastate concentration, momentum, and continuity.

And sometimes a break-in will give you the sinking feeling, *"Where is the nearest table to crawl under."* I remember too well one such moment for me.

As a trial attorney from Michigan, I was attending a Trial Lawyers Association seminar in New Orleans. The guest-speaker was another attorney from Michigan. He was most prominent nationally.

At a reception before the program started, I introduced myself to him. At that time, the Michigan Supreme Court was deciding a crucial case of mine on arbitration. I wanted to hear this attorney's opinion on the issue. He graciously consented. He asked me for details.

I started to give them when suddenly the person in charge of the program walked up. He stood between the attorney and me and blurted out to him: "Harry, I'd like you to meet a friend of mine." He took him by the arm and lead him away.

The Interruption

He did this with arrogant nonchalance. It was replete with a disdainful glance at me. He seemed be saying to me: "Because you're a nobody, I can do this to you." As the saying goes, I felt "about yea high."

That grim moment shows how demeaning interruptions can be. And, how helpless you can be left. In my case, the rude interloper had made his move so quickly that Harry was gone, boom! No time was left for anything but humiliation.

Be a good Samaritan: Let's say that you, Alicia, and Angie are discussing something heard on the news. Alicia starts to express an opinion on the subject, and suddenly Angie cuts her off. Angie then forces you and Alicia to listen to her thoughts on the matter.

When Angie finishes a few minutes later, you turn to Alicia and say: *"Alicia, you were starting to tell us something. I'd like to hear it. Please tell us."*

Saying that to her accomplishes two things:

- You show Alicia that someone does value what she says and thinks. As a result, you restore her self-esteem and soothe her hurt feelings caused by Angie's rudeness. Alicia thinks you're super.

- You adroitly and indirectly teach Angie a lesson. Your "rescue" of Alicia makes it clear to Angie that her interruption was gauche. And if she is a sensible, decent person, she will reflect. She eventually will appreciate the lesson.

If more third parties would do this, it would go a long way to harness interrupters.

Now let's cover some miscellaneous points:

67

Let persons finish even if you've already heard what they're about to tell you. Unless time is critical, don't interrupt someone with *"I've already heard that."* What good does that do? It only causes embarrassment.

In this vein, picture this boorish behavior and its repugnance: In a group of four persons, a showoff-type interrupts another who is telling a joke. The boor breaks in by disclosing the joke's punch lines.

Doing this in effect says: *"Hey stupid, don't you know everyone knows that joke?"* This gets laughs. But they're costly laughs. They turn the victim's face a flushed red.

And you can imagine how low that makes someone feel. Also, for our purposes here, think about where that jerk and those who joined in the laughs now stand with the humiliated person.

So, hear it again! No matter how old the joke or how often you've heard something, patiently, courteously listen again. People will love you for this.

If something comes to mind that relates to what a person is talking about, don't interrupt to make your points about the subject. Save them and make them when the speaker is through.

"But I might forget," you say. Well, if a pen and paper are handy, inconspicuously jot them down while listening. That's the ideal situation.

But most of the time you can't do that. So learn to make mental notes. Doing this with adequate recall is a valuable skill. You have to develop it. It requires a lot of practice. Do it in unimportant scenarios as often as possible.

For example, have someone read something to you for about two minutes. In the first minute, think of something you want to say about that subject after the person is through. Etch it in your mind, and still try to pay attention. It's difficult. But it is great training.

And when it counts sometime, your practicing will pay off. After a speaker has finished, you skillfully will recall points that came to you while you were listening. You will have listened well, not interrupted, and still made your critical points. That's the way to do it.

Never break in with a different matter. Usually when you do this, you regard your subject more important than the speaker's. You commit this vice, because you're plagued with the above mentioned bugaboo, *"If I don't, I'll forget."*

Yes, barring an emergency, don't do it. For example, when the speaker is in the middle of telling you what the lawyer said, don't say: *"Oh, Joe called about the car deal."* Or, *"Hey, look at that gorgeous blue car across the street!"*

And interrupting with that type of abrupt subject change can drive someone up a wall. It can decimate flow, concentration. And it also can throw for a loss the best laid plans of expressing crucial concepts.

This happens too often! You're starting to tell something important. The other person abruptly changes the subject. When the interrupter finishes, you rack your brain for what you were about to say. You draw a blank. You only know that it was something important.

But let's say you do remember it. You still pay a price. You no longer have timing, and this, of course, affects the impact of what you were going to say. Sometimes, you just drop the matter. Yes, that's how costly this type of interruption can be.

Now, if you're one of those who now and then commit this offense, what's the solution? Well, use the skill mentioned above of making written or mental notes. Then, when that can't-wait-matter tempts you to interrupt, hold it! Etch the thought and store it. When the speaker finishes, mention it.

Also, never break in to make an unimportant correction. For example, consider how disruptive and annoying something like this is:

Lydia: *"Remember, last Friday, I was trying to figure out the expense arrangements for the upcoming banquet. Then at 10:00, Jerry walked into the office and said the price for the food should be..."*

Tony (interrupting): *"It was not 10:00. It was 10:30."*

And here's another example, equally irritating and maybe even more so, because it also belittles:

Cynthia: *"I think it's important that we discuss the rules that the president inferred that we should enforce when he talked to us last week. What do you think about number..."*

Sidney (interrupting): *"Cynthia, the correct word is 'implied.' The president **implied** that we should enforce those rules. We're the ones who did the **inferring**. The president did the **implying**. You should learn the difference between those words."*

Obviously, neither correction is important enough to justify interrupting. The fact that Jerry came into the office thirty minutes later than Lydia says doesn't affect the point that she was going to make. And how important is Cynthia's error in diction as to the president's feelings about the rules?

Thus, some people have a penchant to interrupt with pointless corrections. Such rebukes are rude and make speakers feel like two cents.

Avoid sudden diversions of your attention. Another disturbing thing is to suddenly turn your head away from a speaker and look agape at something. You might as well break in with words. The result is the same. You throw sand in the speaker's gears. You're telling her or him that you're no longer listening. Barring emergencies, this is a no-no.

By now, hopefully, you see the common fallout that all adult-interrupters — those who should know better — cause. In varying degrees, their interruptions negatively affect the self-images of persons they break in on.

That's the nub of the abuse. It makes people feel bad about themselves. And this hurts both parties in a relationship, the interrupter and the speaker.

So, curb any tendency to do this. All the above should help you determine if you have this problem. If you do, *work on it!*

How to Improve Your Relationships, Dramatically

Praise,
A not used enough MakeFeelGood!

*Y*ou could argue that this should be part of the *Make Someone's Day* segment. From the perspective that praise can do just that, you'd be right. But between the two MakeFeelGoods is a significant difference that says each should be treated separately.

The *Make Someone's Day* pointer is intended to apply to compliments. You tell persons something nice about them. You like their dresses, suits, comeliness, clothes, their hair styles, et cetera.

Yes, those are compliments. They differ from praise in this way: You usually don't praise persons for things they are, like pretty, handsome, intelligent, and so on. Rather, you praise them for things they do, jobs well done.

So that substantial difference between a compliment and praise is one reason why logically the two should be treated apart. Add to that, praise is so important that it merits ample analysis.

Why is it that significant? Simply because when we don't praise when we should, or don't do it properly, this hurts our ties with others.

Praise for a job well done

The most obvious example, of course, is failure to tell persons when they have done something well. No doubt you have experienced the situation where someone is quick to fault your work but slow to praise it.

If it has the slightest flaw, you'll hear about it. But if your work is beyond reproach, almost perfect, you'll hear nothing.

Unfortunately, that situation is rampant. Silence is considered praise or approval of what you have done.

And what a difference a few words of appreciation can make. Pete: *"Hey, Len, that's a great job on that paper. I like the way you did the first page. That's quite creative!"*

So Len ascends to cloud nine. He feels gooooood! And he also feels that way about Pete.

Contrast that with what usually happens: Pete: *"All right, Len, that's your paper, huh. Let's see, let me read it."*

So he reads it. Then, he says, *"Hmmmmm, OK, thanks."*

That's it. Pete says nothing more. And Len is left twisting in the wind. He thinks his paper is super, but only can guess or rather hope that Pete thinks so too.

Thus, Len doesn't know what to think. He only can rely on Pete's past conduct. When Pete likes his work, Pete's tongue is tied. But when he doesn't like it, he jumps all over it.

So, Len doesn't exactly feel good about the situation. He feels insecure. He's in the dark about how good a job he did.

How does this affect Len and Pete's relationship? Well, it doesn't help, of course.

So, Pete's a dummy for not giving Len a boost. That's because, he really does like the paper. If he didn't, he'd be blasting it. But he just can't bring himself to praise Len.

And why not? What stops the Petes of the world from praising when they should? Well, some reasons parallel those given why people don't compliment as they should. Jealousy and envy come to mind.

Now here's one seemingly screwy hypothesis: Pete's one of many who think like this: *"Boy, I don't want to tell Len how great his paper is. I don't want to give him a big head. He'll become impossible to get along with."*

And how about those who don't praise because they fear being asked for raises? For example, JoAnne doesn't tell the person who cleans her house how much she likes the job done, the super vacuuming, et cetera. She fears that she'll get hit up for more money.

As a result, JoAnne's housekeeper feels unappreciated. So what happens? The housekeeper, in effect, dumps JoAnne by going to work for someone else.

So, don't ignore value received. That's a good way to eventually lose someone's services.

Then there are people who don't praise because it doesn't cross their minds to do it. They're unthinking. They're so preoccupied that they don't recognize the need.

But whatever the reason for not praising, seldom does it stands a test of common sense or logic. That's because a person like Len, the writer of the paper, wants to be appreciated.

Everyone does. So the advisability of praising for a job well done should need little advocacy here.

A don't and a do when praising someone

Too many people commend work that someone has done with words that are too boilerplate, terse. For example, Steve says to his secretary: *"Good letter, Amy."*

That type of short, conclusive comment nags. Amy easily could wonder if Steve means it. Such comments are too mechanical, listless. And they don't meet the needs of persons like Amy. She is foaming at the mouth to know what exactly about her letter Steve likes.

So, let's give Steve another chance. What should he do? He should give her details why he likes the letter.

He easily can do that by making a copy of it and annotating comments on it, like: *"Hey, Amy, that's a tactful way to tell Mark that he needs to get to work."* Or, *"Boy, darn good way to ask for money!"*

When Steve supports his praise with details, he does the following:

- He convinces Amy of his sincerity;
- He shows her that he appreciates the special things she did;
- He motivates her to continue doing well in the future; and
- He makes her feel good about herself and in turn about him.

Thus, you can now see how this type of praising benefits a relationship.

Other ways to praise

Give credit: Has this ever happened to you?:

Jill and Nancy are talking about a nagging problem that Jill has in her job. Nancy suggests a way that Jill solve it by making a certain type of file.

Two weeks later Jill elatedly calls Nancy and says: *"I made a special file. It worked like a charm. My boss is so pleased."*

Jill goes on and on about the matter. But she gives Nancy no credit for the idea.

Finally, Nancy, disgusted, reminds her. And then, of course, Jill says: *"Oh, yes, you did tell me to do that. Thank you so much."* But it's much too late, because Nancy is boiling.

So, the message here is obvious. Having to be reminded to give credit is almost as bad as giving none. So, give it without having to be prompted.

And don't wait too long before doing it: For example, don't do this:

It's the same scenario. After using Nancy's suggestion, Jill goes on and on for about five minutes or so about how well the new file works. But then finally she says, *"Oh, by the way, thanks for the suggestion."*

Though she does this without being prompted by Nancy, she waits much too long to credit her. So, this too miffs Nancy.

Jill immediately should have given credit like this: *"Nancy, thanks to your wonderful suggestion, I finally handled that terrible file problem...."* In other words, the first utterance from Jill's mouth, should be credit.

And why shouldn't she do that? She'll do it eventually. So, why wait? That makes no sense.

So, learn that! Give credit up front. Don't make someone sweat it out and inwardly seethe. When you do that, your name will move to the top of a certain list. And I don't mean a favorite-pal list.

Same point, different twist: Picture this: Jim and Jerry are talking about a murder that local TV stations have been reporting on for weeks. Jerry tells Jim that he thinks the matter will never go to trial. He says the wife will confess at the last minute before the trial starts. But Jim scoffs at the prediction.

Three months pass. Exactly what Jerry predicted, happens. The wife confesses just before trial.

The two pals again discuss the matter. Jerry humbly does not remind Jim of his correct prediction.

He doesn't say: *"Hey, Jim, didn't I tell you that would happen?"* Rather, he patiently waits for Jim to credit him.

Does Jim do that? No. So, Jerry finally abandons his humbleness, and says: *"Hey, don't you remember, I told you that would happen."*

Now, things like this might appear trivial. But in the real world they're anything but. That's because egos are involved. And, as mentioned ad nauseam in this book, in relationships at all times you have to keep egos in mind.

So, let's give Jim another chance to do the right thing:

After the wife's confession hits the news, Jim calls Jerry. He says: *"Gee, Jerry, you sure called the shot in the Smith murder case."* Jerry's face beams like a headlight.

And to Jerry, Jim is Mr. Nice Guy. Their relationship, well, whatever it was, it is now better.

Thus, be sure to credit ideas and thoughts of others that prove correct. You only have to say just a few words like, *"Boy, you sure knew what you were talking about when you said…"* That's all it takes. So ingrain this practice. Do it regularly. People love this.

Snub of major accomplishment

Failing to praise someone for a momentous accomplishment in life is a slighting that smacks of jealousy. Consider the following sketch that depicts well this problem that plaques some relationships:

Wanda and Cindy became friends twenty-five years ago when they were newlyweds. But because of their respective family involvements, raising children et cetera, they have not communicated much.

In their late teens, both Wanda and Cindy's educations and aspirations were interrupted and ended by their marital and parental obligations. Wanda ended up with only a high school diploma, while Cindy finished a little more than a year of college. Each felt cheated, frustrated.

Cindy, however, over the years resolved that some day she was going to finish her education. She had a burning desire to be a family-law attorney.

So six years ago, after her last child had left the nest, Cindy returned to school. She got her undergraduate degree in a hurry. She took as many as twenty-three hours a semester. She graduated magna cum laude.

Then she took on the intimidating challenge of getting into a law school. First, she had to get a decent score on that scary test, the LSAT (Law School Admissions Test).

Law schools use it to judge applicants. She took a preparatory course for the test and practiced religiously.

As a result, she made a respectable score. This enabled her to get into a highly respected law school. She graduated three years later when she was 53.

She then entered a family-law practice and won significant cases. Some were publicized.

So, understandably, you now say, *"Hey, get to the point."* Well, for about the last seven years including Cindy's five years in school, Wanda and she had not talked. So they never had discussed Cindy's return to school.

But Wanda had heard about it from others. And when she did, do you think she called her friend to pat her on the back for her gumption in going back to school? She did not.

And there's more: Several years after graduation, Cindy won a big case. Her local newspaper did a full-page story on her: *It's Never Too Late.*

In essence, the piece related Cindy's history. It detailed all the obstacles she had faced and overcome in returning to school and becoming an attorney. It touted her resolve in fulfilling her dream after years of marriage and children.

Cindy was bursting her buttons. So much so that she sent Wanda a copy of the article. After reading it, did Wanda give Cindy a call? No, she didn't.

It's now two years after that. It's Sunday, and Cindy is spending a weekend in Wanda's city. She calls Wanda and visits her at her home.

While Cindy's there, does Wanda hail her? Of course, you know the answer: It's no.

So now you wonder, does Wanda totally ignore the reality of Cindy's new profession? No, she doesn't go quite that far. But she comes darn close.

That is, she shows practically no interest. Incredibly, she doesn't ask Cindy one question about her law practice. She acts like Cindy works in a supermarket instead of law offices and courtrooms.

And sensing that indifference, Cindy volunteers no information. Her feelings throb with disappointment and dismay.

Wanda's failure to praise her cuts deeply. Wanda's silence seems to shriek: *"Cindy, big whoopee, so you won the Nobel Peace Prize! What do you want me to do, give you a medal?"*

Well, that attitude raises a question. Is Wanda just an odd ball?

No, she isn't. Incredibly, all Cindy's old buddies treat her essentially the same. That is, they give Cindy practically no recognition for her colossal achievements.

But incredulously you ask, *"Are you saying that no one praises her?"* No, some persons certainly do. But the paradox is that those who do are not old chums. They're newcomers in her life.

Yep, blame jealousy

What does this mean? Sadly, it signifies that jealousy keeps old friends from praising when they should. New friends, however, don't have that problem.

Why not? Well, because they have no ties to the past to generate jealousy.

So Wanda, as an old buddy, is glued to the past. And it haunts her. She knows what she was and is. She painfully contrasts that with what Cindy was and is. And she thinks that if she praises Cindy, she's only going to pour salt into her own wound of frustration.

So instead, she employs fiction. She deludes herself that she can purge the impact of her disappointment. She attempts this by ignoring or running away from the reality of what Cindy has become. Wanda wants Cindy's deeds to fade away like dreams.

Well, they won't. And something else won't disappear. That's the hurt Wanda inflicts on Cindy. She just has to be thinking, *"Wanda certainly can't be the friend I had always thought she was. I'm so disappointed that she is not happy for me."*

That, of course, is the pathetic result. Wanda, instead of being delighted for her friend, is depressed.

That's what jealousy does. It destroys relationships. Cindy and Wanda's situation is a case in point.

Can anything be done?

That sad result for Cindy and Wanda raises the question: If you have a tendency to be like Wanda, can you do anything about it?

Well, unfortunately, just about everyone now and then suffers bouts of jealousy. But it doesn't help to sermonize and say, "You shouldn't be jealous. You should be happy for your friend!"

That is should-do advice. It's not practical-can-do advice that is really needed. So, if that's true, what is a you-can-do-it way of dealing with the situation of an old buddy who achieves something fantastic? And because you've always wanted to do the same thing, you're forest green about it.

Well, as said, you can't stem your emotion. But you can try to end run the problem it causes, with self-discipline and some two-and-two-makes-four logic.

Here's what to try: Despite your green eyes, twist your arm and praise.

Convince yourself that you're not going to change your chum's feat or lessen its merit by ignoring it. So, pound that into your noggin as irrefutable logic.

Sum up

Thus, when someone does something that deserves recognition, praise, praise, and praise. Get off that high horse. (At this stage bluntness is in order.)

Practice the never-to-wear-out golden rule. If you were to do something worthy, you certainly would want someone to pat you on the back. So resolve to do it to others.

Do it no matter how envious, or even jealous you are. That person will reciprocate. Both of you will feel good, not only about yourselves but about each other.

Praise, definitely, is a MakeFeelGood!

So, do it!

The "I" Disease,
A MakeFeelBad that's epidemic!

This celebrity has it

*H*ow often on TV have you seen something like this?:

A TV personality is interviewing a celebrity-husband and wife, Ron and Teresa, in their ritzy home in Beverly Hills. She asks them many questions about their life together and interests.

Questioner: *"Ron, are you two satisfied with the size and comfort of your home here in Beverly Hills?"*

Celebrity Ron: *"Well, I think I need a larger house. I need more space. I want each of my kids to have a separate room. I want a bath with a Jacuzzi… [I, I, I blah, blah, blah]."*

So, the "I"s have it. And while Ron's gushing them out, they make Teresa wonder if Ron did marry her. And they make her wonder about a few more things: (1) Aren't those kids that Ron is talking about hers too?; (2) Doesn't she also need a bigger house?; and (3) Doesn't she also want a Jacuzzi?

Well, obviously, Ron's "I" trouble affects Teresa. His

dictionary glaringly lacks two mighty, little words: "we" and "our."

By not using them, he doesn't exactly make Teresa feel like climbing a mountain. Nor does she now want to put their marriage certificate into a gold-embossed frame.

But judging Ron charitably, he doesn't realize that he's sick. He's in the grips of that dreadful affliction, the "I" disease.

This banker has it

And so is Tony, the bank employee, in the next illustration. Just about all of us now and then run into his type:

Tony is a customer-service representative of Good Times Bank. He is talking with Gene Smith, who has a checking and savings account there.

Gene is trying to get the bank to let him access both accounts through his computer. But because of some requirement that Gene doesn't meet, Tony is telling him he won't let him do it.

And here's how Tony does that: *"Mr. Smith, I am not going to authorize that. I am not going to let you do that. I simply cannot let you draw from both accounts. You don't meet my requirements. I'm sorry."*

Well, the first question is, when did Tony buy the bank? And the second question, when did he write the bank's rules? The third question that logically follows is: Did Good Times Bank train Tony before turning him loose on customers? Those questions say it all, don't they?

And you and I also say: *"Hey, Tony, you too, should add the words: 'we' and 'our' to your dictionary and vernacular. If you don't, you'll never come close to running a bank, much less owning it."*

This chairman of the board has it

Now here's another: This involves a person whose status says he should know better.

The legislature of a large state is investigating a trade. Numerous small companies are involved. They are threatened with harsh penalties for alleged illegal conduct and collusion. The legislators propose a settlement. The companies, however, reject it.

Following the rejection, the chairman of one of the larger companies holds a news conference. He seems to be speaking for the trade, all the companies. He says, *"To end this thing, if you think I'm going to go down the legislative halls pleading, forget it. I'm not going to do that. And I'm not going to do… [this] and I'm not going to do [that]… [I, I, I, I, blah, blah, blah]"*

So here too, the "I"s have it. They flourish in Mr. Chairman's sentences. It is as if he owns and controls all the companies. And you wonder how persons from the other corporations must feel about him after this press conference.

It turns out that he is just another person who seems to have never heard of the little word, "we." And to think that this man has become chairman of that prosperous company without learning how to use that potent little word. That's incredible, right?

One answer: His family owns the company. So, he didn't have to climb the ladder.

Why?

Anyway, what makes persons use seemingly egocentric words? In their defense, many decent people speak that way.

So we can't chalk it up to something villainous about these users.

Then, to what can we attribute this abuse? Well, usually, persons' misuse of "I"s and "my"s indicates an image problem. Their self-esteem is in the pits. They want to feel important. And they evidently delude themselves that they're accomplishing this when they misuse those little words.

And some people are just mindless. It just doesn't occur to them how wrong it is to use words that way. If only they'd do what you're doing: That is, if only they would read this book. Wham, they'd mend their ways pronto.

Then, we have persons like Ron, the celebrity in the TV interview. He's probably a bad apple, a revolting egomaniac. His wife, Teresa, must have a dubious individuality. Moreover, Ron's words just have to affect her self-esteem. It must be in a deep hole, and it's likely to stay there. What else, living with someone like Ron?

And how about that chairman! Boy, can you imagine having to work for that guy? His words parade the arrogance of power.

So it's obvious, one easily can damage a relationship by misusing tiny words that carry wallops. The "I" disease can cause someone in essence to say to the other: *"You don't belong."* Or *"This is all mine; I'm not sharing this with you."* Wow! Such messages do undermine bonds. They're MakeFeelBads!

Can you do anything?

Hopefully, you don't suffer from this malady. But if you do, take some pills and call your doctor, the one who prescribes words.

But seriously, do something. Admitting to yourself that you have the problem probably will be enough. This will force you to be more careful in your use of, "I" and "my." And you'll learn that "we," and "our" are the way to go.

Thus, now you know. The manner in which you use these little-bitty words can have an enormous impact on your ties with people.

So watch them!

Build Self Esteem
Ask for an Opinion or Advice.

*T*his is a MakeFeelGood because usually, when you ask someone for an opinion or advice about something important, indirectly, you are giving that person a message. You are saying this: *"You are intelligent. I trust you. I know you will only tell me what you think is best for me. I respect what you say and think."*

These implicitly said things have a most positive impact on that other person's self-image. Few things can buoy it more.

And, of course, when you do that for someone, you're bound to improve the relationship between you. That person appreciates your trust and confidence.

You must really want help

But your request must be sincere, genuine. You must not have Johnny's mind-set in the following skit:

He is in his third year at the university studying accounting. He is heavily in debt from student loans. He's struggling. He is tired of skimping, barely getting by.

In contrast, Johnny sees his high school buddies doing well financially. Each has a snazzy, new sports car, nice clothes, and a cool apartment with cozy, new furniture. Rather than going to college after high school, they took full time-factory jobs.

So, Johnny is envious. He wishes that he had done the same. He now wants to quit school and get a job at the factory where his buddies work.

But he just doesn't feel right doing this without first talking to his father. As you will see, he deludes himself that he wants his dad's opinion.

So, he approaches his dad and tells him what he's thinking about doing. The father listens patiently. But as you probably guess, he disagrees with the plan.

As best he can, for all the obvious reasons, Johnny's father tactfully, gently tries to persuade him to stay in school.

But Johnny reacts to his dad's counsel like many people do to advice. He argues about it. He shows that he really doesn't want guidance.

What he really wants is approval or confirmation that he's doing the right thing. And when he doesn't get it, he shows resentment and defiance.

Thus, it goes without saying that this type of exchange between two persons does little for their bond. So, the lesson is, don't seek counsel from someone close to you unless you sincerely want it.

In other words, you should not do what Johnny does. That is, don't solicit support for something you've already decided to do.

Rather, you should graciously seek and accept the person's counsel for its value. And though you might disagree with it, you still want it. In any case, you appreciate the help and respect the advice.

But respecting it doesn't mean that you have to follow it. It just means that you give it thorough consideration.

And when you do that, you really do tell such persons trying to help you that you trust and respect them. You value what they say.

This in turn tells them that they are important persons in your life. You reinforce their self-worth.

> *And for that, they love or like you more than they did before. That's the ball game.*

Talking Down

A Bad, Bad MakeFeelBad!

*T*his is a classic way to undermine or put to task a relationship. When one person belittles the other by talking down, the bond between the two just has to suffer.

This is because, in effect, the put-downer is lowering the self-worth of the other person. It is done by delivering implied messages that can run the gamut from *"You're stupid"* to *"I'm smarter than you,"* as well as other negatives in-between.

The following are common ways to put someone down. Hopefully, you're not doing any. But beware, because you could be doing some without realizing that you do.

Saying the obvious

Sisters, Hillary and Tess, are talking about Bill, Tess' husband, who has been ill.

Hillary: *"Boy, Bill looks much worse to me. His skin has a sickly look."*

Tess: *"Geez, Hillary, whatever you do, don't tell Bill that!"*

Wham! That goes over like a lead balloon. Hillary feels insulted, hurt. She heatedly answers, *"Of course not!"* And she reflects to herself bitterly, *"Gosh, Tess, I'm shocked that you think I could be that stupid."* Thus, this exchange leaves things a bit touchy between the sisters.

But let's change the skit for the better. Here are two new scenarios: In each, Tess uses her head. She avoids offending her sister:

Scenario one: Let's say Tess realizes that Hillary is a normally intelligent, sensitive person. So, Tess knows that Hillary would never repeat her comment to Bill. Thus, Tess doesn't have to say a word to her. And she doesn't.

Scenario two: Let's speculate that Hillary really is a bit dense. So Tess does have a legitimate concern. But she still avoids hurting Hillary's feelings by using tact. Here's how:

After Hillary's comment about Bill's distressful appearance, Tess says: *"Hillary, you're right. But I'm so glad that you're such a considerate person. I just know you would never say anything like that to Bill or within an earshot of him."* Hillary picks up on the suggestion and says: *"Oh yes, I won't say a word."*

Bottom line: ***Don't the say the obvious.*** But if you have to, sugarcoat it with finesse as in that last skit.

Beware of Dog, the dogmatist, that is

Know-it-all, over positive persons can be insufferable. They also can put dampers on their relationships. Why and how? Read on:

Jody (to Emily, her next door neighbor): *"Yesterday, my son, Leo, moved out of his apartment at the complex on Interstate 45. His lease had expired. He hopes to get his $1,000 security deposit back."*

Emily: *"Well, he can kiss that goodbye."*

Jody: *"What do you mean? He's entitled to it. He left the place in beautiful condition. I saw it."*

Emily: *"**I tell you** he's not going to get it back. **I know!** That outfit never gives money back. I've heard a lot about that place. And furthermore they don't have to give it back. **That's the law!** The landlords have all the cards. **Everyone knows that!"***

As you can see, Emily is a typical dogmatist. She tries to give the impression that she's knowledgeable. She talks as authoritatively as a lawyer who specializes in landlord and tenant law. Moreover, typically, like most dogmatists, she states her conclusive, overly positive opinion without being fully informed. She knows nothing about Leo's lease.

But aside from all the obvious reasons why no one should be a dogmatist, being so talks down to the other person. This can damage a relationship.

This happens because the dogmatist disparages the other person's intelligence or knowledge. And that's exactly what Emily does in our skit. She, in effect, says to Jody, *"Hey, Dummy, don't you know this?"*

Now, what does that do to Jody's self-worth? How does she now feel about Emily? The obvious answers say it all.

But you ask, *"How can I avoid being dogmatic, when I'm really positive about something?"* That's a fair question. Let's answer it with another example:

Skip and Tim are classmates and best friends. Skip tells Tim that their professor in economics, while discussing a practice problem, told the class that a certain debt was $100.

But Tim is absolutely positive that she said only $50. It is a critical point for their final exam.

So, here's how Tim handles it without being a dogmatist:

He hedges a bit. That is, Tim qualifies his statement. He prefaces it like this: *"Gee, Skip, as I understand you, you're saying the professor said the debt was $100. Well, I could have misheard* [the hedge], *but at the lecture, I wrote in my notes that she had said $50. Let me show you my notebook."*

By saying it that way, Tim is not putting Skip down. And at the same time, he's not compromising his position. He's only conceding a reality: That where a human's act is involved, seldom can anyone be one-hundred percent sure about anything.

So even when you're so positive that you'd bet the barn, qualify and hedge. You can't go wrong.

Besides, you won't be barking like a dog, a dogmatist that is.

You be the dummy!

You probably see the abuse that follows more on TV than you do in your world. Nevertheless, it's a put-downer worthy of mention as an ounce of prevention. Here's an example:

TV announcer: *"Let's say you notice ABCD stock in today's market selling for ten dollars a share. Last week it was five dollars, and yesterday, eight dollars. So, tomorrow morning you think you should latch onto a couple hundred shares and make some big bucks. Right? Well, think again! You're wrong!"*

Now, it's difficult to understand how the great minds of television allow that type of thing. But they do. The announcer, in essence, is assuming that the viewers have poor judgment and untactfully is telling them just that. Or, arguably, the announcer is saying, *"Hey, dummies, you'd better get a handle on this."*

So, how should something like this be done? That is, you want to warn someone important to you about something that's not what it seems. And you don't want to offend.

The answer is simple. Always make yourself the dummy, the fall-guy. Let's have the TV announcer do that in a new script:

TV Announcer: *"Suppose in today's paper I notice ABCD stock… So, I think tomorrow morning I should… Well, I'd better think again, because I'm wrong!"*

Thus, the listener is not the dumbbell with the poor judgment. Rather, it's the announcer. He puts the finger on himself.

So, when it's necessary to make somebody look bad, make that person yourself. Yes, to make a point or teach a lesson, never pick on the other person in your relationship. That's a put-down, a MakeFeelBad. Instead, you be the stupe.

And being the stupe, sometimes means you really aren't. The other person is. But the last thing you want to do is say so. Here's a typical way that people in relationships do this to each other, much, much too often:

Jenny: *"Tommy, now take I-10 west to the Addicks*

exit. Get off there and go left or south to Bellaire. Then you turn west. About a mile down the road, you'll see McDonald's on the right. My car is in McDonald's left parking lot."

Tommy: "*Let's see now, I take I-10 to the west and get off at Addicks. I go south to Bellaire and then turn back towards downtown, till I see McDonald's on the right where your car is.*"

Jenny: "*Wait a minute, Tommy, I didn't say that! I told you to turn west on Bellaire, away from down-town. Now pay attention. You're gonna get lost, darn it!*"

Well, obviously Jenny is talking down to Tommy. She in effect is saying, "*Hey, Stupid, why don't you listen like you should?*"

Now contrast that response from Jenny with this one:

Jenny: "*Gee, Tommy, I'm so sorry, I must have goofed. I meant to say turn west on Bellaire, away from down-town, not toward it. Please forgive me.*"

Can't you just see the difference that second approach can make? Both methods correct Tommy's mistake. But the first approach decimates his feelings. And the second, well, you get the message.

Try to eliminate "You must understand" or "Keep in mind"

Change those phrases to: "We must understand" or "We must keep in mind."

That word "we," means you **too** have to follow the same principle or advice. You **too** have the same concern and need.

By doing this, you identify with others. You make them feel closer to you. You're human just like they are.

And it's amazing how many important people in the world don't do this. They say "You must," "You should" instead of "We must," and "We should." Arguably, this makes it look like they feel superior to the persons to whom they're talking. The counsel they're offering doesn't apply to themselves. They're above need. That's not true, of course. But that's the perception. It's another way of talking down to people, a MakeFeelBad that's easy to remedy.

So, remember, unless you're in a teaching or counseling role, such I am in trying to help you with this book, use: *"We must"* or *"We should,"* instead of "You must" or "You should."

Watch those big words, foreign phrases, jargon

Try not to use words or talk in terms that other persons might not understand. Not many things make people feel dumber than having other persons talk over their heads.

These persons use big words, foreign phrases, or jargon. Or they unreasonably assume knowledge that listeners don't have. And without such knowledge they are going to be lost and frustrated.

Often listeners blame themselves. Their self-worth plummets. Of course, the problem really lies with the speakers. They brandish their learning and in the process punish listeners.

Some such talkers are plain showoffs. They're braggers who try to impress people and usually succeed. But it's another story as to what they do to their relationships.

In contrast to braggers, some people use abstruse language unthinkingly. They don't deserve as much blame. That's the good news. But the bad news is that they can wreak just as much damage to the self-esteem of others. They often use jargon or special business-language.

For example, let's say, Wilma, a real estate agent, is telling her neighbor, Darlene, about a new property that she is trying to sell. She says, *"Tomorrow I am going to show the owner 'comps.'"*

Darlene, not in the real estate business, does not know that a "comp" is the price for which a similar house sold. So, Darlene has to decide whether to ask Wilma what the term means, or just let it go by.

The situation makes Darlene feel uneducated, ignorant. The fact that her neighbor is only being addlebrained does not help. Snow-white intentions don't matter.

But does that mean you should never use special words and language? In other words, you can't use such things unless the person you're talking to is at your level? After all, some terms are necessary to communicate concepts.

No, it doesn't mean that. What it means is this: You should continually try to put yourself in the place of the other person. Were you that person, would you understand this word or jargon? If you have doubt, you should define it. Here's one way:

Tom (to Mary, his close co-worker): *"Mary, some people are pedants. [As you know, pedants are those persons who like to show off their education.] Do you know any?"*

Now, let's suppose, Tom doesn't give the bracketed definition, and Mary doesn't know what a pedant is. The context of Tom's words tells her nothing. So, she embarrassingly has to ask Tom what a pedant is, or shoot in the dark.

If she takes a chance and answers, *"Yes, I do know some,"* Tom is likely to pursue the matter. She enters even deeper water. And eventually, her ignorance surfaces.

So, her safe answer appears to be, "No." But that could end the conversation.

Thus, in this situation, whatever Mary answers, she feels lost and maybe even a little stupid. And it's Tom's fault.

Now consider how much better things are for Mary if Tom follows the above bracketed recommendation. He says those magical-fourteen-additional words, the definition. Mary can respond intelligently, comprehensively. And most important, Tom does not brutalize her ego.

But what if Mary does know what a pedant is? Won't Tom offend her by defining it?

No, not if he does it using that prefatory clause, *"As you know."* This way, he's assuming that she does know the word. But in case she doesn't, he's helping her without talking down to her. He's not saying something like, *"Mary, you should learn that word, it means…"*

So there you have it. It's a can't-lose way of using a word that might not be understood.

In sum, you should always keep in mind who your audience is. And, as said, whenever you have a doubt whether something will be understood, you should explain or define it.

This also applies to words with foreign derivatives like the following:

- *Fait accompli* (something done that can't be undone)
- *Cause celebre* (a widely publicized court case)
- *Coup* (something sudden that gets results)
- *Faux pas* (a social blunder)

Those are but a few. They are over the head of many persons. So you should define them in a tactful way like Tom does in the example above. You can't err doing this. But you sure can if you don't.

The "you know" bit

The use of this phrase is hardly ever justified. Often you hear it as an annoying speech-filler or pause: *"I went to the store, you know, to buy some shoes for her, you know."*

But that use doesn't talk down. The use that does talk down, is this: *"The schools close on the first, you know." "Your daughter's an adult, you know."*

A listener easily can take offense from such comments. The "you know" part has a chiding aspect. It's almost as if a speaker is saying, *"I'm surprised you don't know this,"* or, *"Are you so dumb that you don't know this simple thing?"*

And when the matter is something so basic like one's daughter being an adult, the comment really miffs. No one needs to be told the age of a daughter.

But suppose you need to emphasize the daughter's age. How do you do it without affronting?

You say something like this: *"And, as we both well know, Joe, your daughter is an adult."* This wording is innocuous.

Prefatory phrases like that can really help. They provide finesse. Here are more examples:

- *"**As you know,** Hilda, the schools close on the first."*
- *"**As you've probably heard on the news,** John, the school board meets tonight."*
- *"Pete, **I'm sure you realize** that we don't have much time."*
- *"Mary, **no doubt you've considered this, but…**"*
- *"Teresa, **with your memory, I know you won't forget** to call Joe, right?"*

By using such phrases, you won't talk down by assuming that other persons are unknowledgeable. Rather, you will assume the best about them; that they are alert, up-to-date, informed, et cetera. You are giving them the benefit of doubt. They will appreciate it.

So you should get such prefatory phrases down pat. Using them can make enormous differences in how persons feel about you. Try them. You'll see.

Help persons understand you

And keep in mind, that not talking down, also means that you should do anything you can to help people understand what you're saying to them. Being able to follow things told them is a critical factor in persons' opinions of themselves.

So, if you sometimes talk to people in a way that they can't grasp what you're saying, this can make them feel stupid. And, of course, that's not the way you want important-to-you persons to feel about themselves after contact with you. That's a MakeFeelBad.

Now, you can prevent that. You discipline yourself to use the KISS principle: "Keep it simple stupid." The implication is: *You're the one who is stupid* if you don't make concepts simple when you talk or explain things. That's a darn good rule! So, keep repeating it to yourself and try to practice it.

Finally, try to follow all the above suggestions. They'll keep you from talking down to those who mean much to you.

Gratitude,
A much overlooked MakeFeelGood!

*W*ords of gratitude are so simple to say. Yet for many people, uttering them is a real chore. The words balk, don't want to come out. As a result, few persons say them as often as they should.

This lacking probably evolves from habits ingrained in childhood. Youngsters, of course, receive gifts and services coming out their ears. They expect and take such things for granted.

This attitude easily could carry over into adulthood. It could account for why many persons fail to express gratitude like they should.

Such failures are missed opportunities to make others feel good. And the converse can result. Yes, those who are owed gratitude and don't get it, feel neglected, unappreciated. And you can imagine how they feel about those who can't be bothered to show some appreciation.

Sometimes a bad result is immediate. Some teenagers discover this the hard way. They think it's "uncool" to show appreciation or enthusiasm about things done for them by adults.

To these kids, the "cool" way to respond is to act like a deadpan. Their attitude reeks. Its says the world owes them a living.

Here's an example:

Dad (to his fourteen-year-old daughter and two of her friends): *"Ellen, how would you like it if I took you guys down to Duffy's and get you each a banana split? Then I'll drop you off at the mall for a movie."*

Ellen: *"If you want."*

Dad: *"Well, don't do me any favors, Ellen, I've got other things to do. Just forget it."*

As you can see, at 14, Ellen is learning that dire results can evolve immediately from acting like an ingrate. Appearing cool to her friends, cost all three youngsters a banana split and a movie.

Thus, not showing gratitude can be a real turnoff. If only Ellen had said, *"Oh boy, Dad, what a deal, thank you, thank you, thank you!"*

Sometimes that's the kind of exuberance necessary to show genuine gratitude. A hollow, boilerplate "thank you" won't cut it. It's almost as bad as Ellen's "if you want."

But if a simple "thank you" is said with obvious, effusive earnestness, it can suffice. For example, a smiling, beaming face says, "Thannnk youuuuuu!" Applicable here is the adage, "It's not what you say, but how you say it."

Yes, that makes a difference. That's what shows your sincerity. And if you do it right, you only need to say two words, "thank you."

But sometimes, spoken words don't suffice

At times, merely expressing appreciation verbally doesn't do the trick. It can be too shallow, impotent. You need to write it.

For example, when people give you thoughtful gifts, verbal thanks seldom suffice. Or when persons go a second mile in rendering you courtesies, almost always you can show more sincerity with written expressions of gratitude.

Legend has it they helped elect a president

Attesting to this, is how former President George H. Bush is said to have used handwritten-thank-you notes during his presidential campaign. He was most diligent in sending them to persons who had treated him well or afforded him courtesies. This practice earned him much praise for his graciousness and considerateness.

It likely also won him many followers that he otherwise might not have had. And when things got tough in his party primaries, this support came through. And that in turn helped him win his eventual victory at the polls. Yes, that's the presidential legend about the power of putting those two little words, "thank you," in writing.

So, express gratitude regularly, verbally or in writing as circumstances dictate. Yes, you have to show sincere, adequate appreciation to those who do things for you. It can make quite a difference in your relationships with them.

How to Improve Your Relationships, Dramatically

Little White Lies

Take them, or leave them?

*Y*es, you decide, should you use them as MakeFeelGoods?

Maybe you're one of those who believe that lies, untruths deliberately told, no matter how teeny-weeny, are never justified.

Many persons feel that way. It is a principle that deserves respect.

So, if that is your belief, read no further. Skip this MakeFeelGood and proceed to number eleven.

But let's say your mind is open. You're willing to be shown how sometimes a little white lie is a wonderful MakeFeelGood. It's beneficial.

But to be considered that, the white lie must pass the truth-is-not-necessary test. This is because sometimes truth is necessary. If health, safety, or some other important matter is involved, the truth tactfully should be told.

But here, we're only discussing white lies for situations where a truthful answer is not needed. The truth will serve no purpose other than make someone feel bad. The following is typical:

Thelma is talking to her mother, Bernice, who is in her fifties and has put on a few pounds.

Bernice: *"Thelma, do you think I'm fat?"*

Thelma: *"Absolutely not, Mom, you look great."*

Or say it goes like this:

Bernice: *"Thelma, yesterday I was 55, do you think I look that old?"*

Thelma: *"No, Mom. Actually, you look like you're in your late forties."*

In these examples, Thelma is helping her mom avoid reality with a couple of white lies. The last thing her mother would want to hear is the truth.

But let's change the situation. Say Thelma belongs to the Always Tell The Truth Club. How will she respond to those questions from her mom?

Will she tell the truth? Will she say?: *"Well, you do look a tad hefty."* And, *"Yeah, Mom, to be honest, you do look your age."*

No, of course, she won't give those answers. They would hurt too much.

So, what will she do? Well, she'll likely evade the questions.

She'll say something like this: *"Gee, Mom, let's not talk about silly things like that. By the way, did Bill call today?"*

But when Thelma does that, isn't she, in essence, still answering with the brutal truth? That is, she's indirectly telling her mom that she's fat or looks her age.

Yes, Thelma's unwillingness to answer implies those messages. And they cut.

In short, such exchanges occur often in the real world. And they argue strongly for little white lies.

So, whenever you face Thelma's predicament, you have three choices:

(1) Tell the truth;

(2) Evade; or

(3) Tell a white lie.

The first two are MakeFeelBads. The third is a MakeFeelGood.

You decide.

I rest my case.

How to Improve Your Relationships, Dramatically

The Big "C"s,

Courtesy - Consideration

Are always MakeFeelGoods!

*T*his is one of those areas that are just plain-common sense. You likely will say to much of this, "I know that." Agreed. You do know many of the things that follow.

But you need to be reminded of them. They are so important that you should etch them with indelible chalk on your mental blackboard.

Do this, because few things can make other persons feel better toward you than affording them utmost courtesy and consideration. And treating special people in your world that way is so compelling!

With this in mind, let's review some dos and don'ts that involve the big Cs. They're matters that deserve special attention:

Make eye contact with persons with whom you converse. This is a courteous, considerate thing to do.

But some of us have an innate problem doing this. It's a type of shyness. If you are one of these persons, you can overcome it. It's a matter of disciplining yourself and practicing.

One method to overcome the problem is to focus on the other person's forehead, just above the eyes. When you're able to do that regularly, then you can try focusing directly on eyes.

By dividing your learning into those two stages or steps, the problem is easier to conquer. It's a method that works well.

But maybe you don't have a problem making eye contact. And all you need is this pointer about its extreme importance so you'll do it without fail.

Yes, it's critical, because, as mentioned, it's a necessary courtesy. And most importantly, it encourages trust and confidence.

But perhaps it really shouldn't be so darn important. Maybe we read too much into doing or not doing it.

Con artists, no doubt, are most proficient at making eye contact. So to trust persons because they impress you with penetrating, incessant eye contact, doesn't seem provident.

But that conclusion is not pertinent, because with this particular mannerism, perception is reality. Too many people will judge you by whether or not you do it. You're shifty if you don't, and a rock if you do. And they feel the same way about you whether or not you have a vice-like hand shake. Like it or not, that's the real world.

So, a word to the wise: Make a habit of maintaining almost constant eye contact!

Talk to everyone in the group. When you're talking to more than one person, try to share eye contact (there it is again) with each person. Focus on one set of eyes for a number of seconds, then move to another set. In that manner, divide your attention equally among all persons.

Doing this is such an important consideration! But few people do it.

When it's not done, well, it sure can lower the self-image of someone quickly. Consider the following example:

Marty is talking to his brother, Louis, and his wife, Shirley. They are having dinner together. Marty is telling them his opinion about friendships in the workplace. Though supposedly he is talking to both persons, his eye contact and attention are focused solely on Louis.

It's almost as if Shirley is not there. She thinks that Marty considers her either a dummy or a child, incapable of understanding and unworthy of his attention. This puts her self-worth in the pits. That scenario happens often. Guard against it, and always try to spread your attention and eye contact equally.

If you make a practice of this, you'll be flabbergasted at the results. You'll see a substantial difference in how well those in a group will react to what you say.

Always introduce a person accompanying you. If you don't, you knock for a loop the self-worth of your companion. Here's what can happen:

Leo and Marlene, husband and wife, are at Leo's company-cocktail party. While Leo knows everyone there, Marlene knows no one. With her at his side, several times Leo approaches co-workers and their spouses. He converses with them. But each time he fails to introduce Marlene.

She, of course, is peeved. She feels that Leo regards her as a fixture, unimportant. She lacks identity as his wife.

And who knows what some of Leo's co-workers might imagine her to be. This offends her.

Now one excuse that persons like Leo have for not introducing is that they don't remember names. At times, this happens to everyone.

Well, a way around that exists. It's a technique that serves two purposes: (1) It avoids offending companions, and (2) it remedies a memory loss. Here's how it would work in the situation of Leo and Marlene:

They are approached by Smitty and Tess, Leo's two new co-workers. He just met them yesterday.

Leo: *"Well, hi there, newcomers. Hey, I'd like you to meet my wife, Marlene." (Leo now pauses)*

Tess: *"Great, I'm Tess James, and this is Smitty Corrigan. It's so nice to meet you, Marlene."*

With this method, Leo gets Tess' help without emphasizing embarrassingly that he can't remember her and Smitty's names. And when Leo doesn't state their names to Marlene, it only appears like a minor oversight.

That doesn't say to Tess and Smitty, *"Hey, you're such nobodies, I've forgotten your names."* And, of course, it doesn't belittle Marlene, by saying: *"You don't rate an intro."*

Add to that, Leo now knows the other couple's names. No one knows that he had forgotten them.

Oh sure, it's better to be good with names and not have such problems. But that's not real world for many of us. So this technique bails us out. It's easy and prevents hurt feelings on all sides.

So, for whatever reason, those who don't introduce companions commit discourtesies that hurt relationships. If you have this tendency, take it to task. And if your memory is the problem, use the above technique. It works well.

Now, you might not agree with this suggestion, because you might be one of those who think it's a dated custom. But if you're a man, you can make a woman in your life, whether she's your boss, co-worker, wife, sister, mother, aunt, fiancee, or whoever feel like a million. Show her courtesies, like the following:

- Hold open car doors and other doors for her.
- Rise when she enters the room.
- Rise when she arrives at or leaves a table.
- Pull out and hold the chair for her when she attempts to sit down at a table.
- Permit her to enter a room or other opening before you.

Such gestures please most women. They feel valued, respected.

But true, some people feel that such gestures are not necessary. But to build better relationships with most women, they can be a real plus.

You have everything to gain and nothing to lose by affording the special women in your life these courtesies. But this is opinion.

And as the saying goes, "Opinions are like bellybuttons; everyone has one." Moreover, reasonable minds can disagree.

Translate foreign language conversations for companions. Suppose you're at a gathering with someone important to you. You speak Spanish fluently, but your companion speaks nary a word of it. A third person approaches and starts speaking to you in Spanish. For your companion, you should translate each side of the conversation.

Ask the Spanish speaker to pause a bit after each of you talks. This will give you time to turn to your companion and translate.

If you don't do this, your companion could feel:

- You and the other person are talking about her or him;
- You and the other person are showing off; or
- Like a dunce.

Needless to say, all three are downers. They hurt a relationship. They result from inconsiderateness and discourtesy. And it's a situation that is so easy to remedy. Simply translate everything.

This will make things challenging, lively, and interesting for everyone.

Being considerate also means not being a flake: This should go without mention. But so many persons are unreliable. And this is so damaging to a relationship. A commitment has to be taken with a grain of salt.

In contrast, how secure and confidence-inspiring it is to have a bond with someone you regard as a rock. When a commitment is made, it's as good as done. Promises mean something. That's so important.

Yes, reliability is a priceless trait. Some persons are blessed with it by nature. The rest have to work at it. They can become reliable with practice and desire. And the motivation can be how much this will improve their bonds with others.

Here's another potent way to be considerate: Janice tells Jeannene: *"As soon as I hear from Bob about the time we're going to meet tomorrow, I'll give you a call. He promised he would call this afternoon and let me know."*

At 5:30 that afternoon, Janice telephones her friend, and says: *"Jeannene, gee, I want you to know that Bob did not call me. So, I'm trying to find him. I'll get back with you tonight, and let you know if I had any luck."*

Unfortunately, in this world, many, if not most, persons in Janice's shoes would not have made that 5:30 call to Jeannene. They would think, *"Well, I didn't hear from Bob. I only said I'd call her if I heard from him."* And, of course, technically that's right.

But it's the wrong way to be right. It's like being dead right in the cemetery. It's counterproductive to maintaining a good relationship with someone. It's definitely not being considerate. We all know how unnerving it is to be waiting for a phone call that doesn't come. You wonder and you wonder.

So, consider that anxiousness, how it feels, and always, always report back to persons who are expecting to have information by a certain time. Hearing something, though not fulfilling, is better than hearing nothing. You at least eliminate the thought that the matter has been overlooked; that someone doesn't give a hoot.

In essence, this is nothing but common-sense courtesy. And for this MakeFeelGood, that's the name of the game.

*Now here are some blatant discourtesies
that can offend and berate:*

Don't criticize within an earshot of others. Criticism always is hard to stomach. And when it's not done privately, it can be destructive. No matter how well intentioned, its value can be lost when others can hear it. The criticizer makes the criticized feel "yeah high." And you can imagine how this affects the tie between the two. So, make it an absolute: Always do touchy things, like criticizing, or even making suggestions, in private.

When in a group, never take part in poking fun at or mocking one member under the guise of, *"We're just teasing."* Few things are more humiliating.

Sure, it might seem great fun at the time, but it's costly in feelings. The game is not worth the candle.

Because it's so wrong, you should even consider rising to the defense of the one being ridiculed. Say something like this: *"Gee, I really don't think this is fair or proper. Let's talk about something else."*

But if you feel that you can't go that far, at least, in some way show that you are not participating and do not approve. In either case, you'll stand tall with the person being mocked.

Add this one: It's a group-situation that reeks of rudeness, inconsiderateness. It happens often:

Bill, Joe, and Sally are lunching. The men enter into an extensive, intense conversation about a problem at work. Sally, doesn't work there. She knows nothing about the matter. Thus, she feels left out. She's the fifth wheel.

Now, other than making such a private conversation

taboo, is there another way? Yes. If Bill and Joe's subject could interest an outsider, they should have Sally participate. That means they should explain the problem to her. Then, the three should exchange opinions. Often an impartial outsider can see things that insiders cannot. This can make a lively conversation And Bill and Joe will be saying to Sally: *"We respect you and value your presence."* Needless to say, this is a MakeFeelGood.

An annoying, maddening discourtesy: You might think this one belongs in the *Gratitude,* MakeFeelGood section. But because it's such an egregious breach of manners that fosters, breeds so much ill-will, it belongs here.

It comes into play when people can't be bothered to write personal-thank you notes.

A good example is wedding gifts. At considerable cost, you attend an out-of-town wedding of your business associate's daughter. You really do not know her or her husband-to-be. You're attending as a courtesy to your associate.

You also send the couple a lovely gift. It costs you a bundle.

Other than a mechanical, *"Hi, thanks for coming,"* your associate shows no appreciation for your attendance. This business person just has to realize the expense and inconvenience you incurred.

And do the newlyweds pen you a note for the costly gift you gave them? You can guess the answer to that, it's no!

Of course, many newlyweds, if not most, do the right thing. They send thank-you notes for wedding gifts. But, incredibly, a sizable percentage of couples do not. They always have the old standby, *"We're just so busy."*

In the example above, should you pardon the couple because of their youth? Should you excuse them because they really don't know you?

No, is the answer to both questions. If this couple is old enough to get married, they're adults. As such, they should know better and have the decency to send a thank-you note.

And what about your associate? Should that person be excused because, technically, it was the responsibility of the daughter to send a thanks? No, that doesn't wash either. Why? Well, because, as an obligation and courtesy to you, the associate should have made sure that the daughter did the proper thing.

So, in no way can your associate's oversight be excused! It's a blatant discourtesy, an inconsiderateness that unfortunately is rampant among too many persons. And because it makes someone just plain mad, it's relationship-damaging.

Moreover, it's damage that could be so easily prevented with a postage stamp and five minutes of time.

Such conduct makes you wonder, how can people be so dense, lazy, unthinking, or whatever? Good question!

In short, *try to walk in the moccasins of persons in relationships with you.* Decide were you they, what courtesies and considerations you would like to be afforded. That benchmark, combined with the counsel offered above, will help you determine what changes you need to make in your conduct.

"You're Picking on Me"
is a MakeFeelBad!

*I*n essence, that's what you're saying when you try to defend or justify a mistake that you've made. Yes, that's the message you give when you're defensive. Here's an illustration:

Sam is a vice president of a neighborhood investment club. A few days ago, he submitted an expense report to Tony, the club's president. Tony finds a $10,000 error in the total:

Tony: *"Sam, would you believe it, but the bottom line here is off by $10,000. I checked the figures two times and had my wife do it a third time."*

Sam: *"Well, if we had a decent calculator in the office, maybe I would be able to give you the right figure. And the heat in there! I don't know how you can expect anyone to do anything right in that oven. Besides, you don't give me enough time to get these reports out. Just try doing it yourself in those time frames."*

Sam's defensiveness is indirectly telling Tony, that he, Sam:

- Resents being told that he made a mistake;
- Wants to blame Tony; and
- Wants to make Tony feel bad for having pointed out the mistake.

That scenario shows obvious downsides to being defensive. A person like Sam:

- Puts down the other person;
- Challenges that person's fairness and judgment;
- Wrongfully switches blame to that person; and
- Discourages future help or suggestions, thereby impeding future opportunities to learn, improve.

Add to that, the main point for our purposes here: Persons acting defensively, like Sam, hurt relationships. In the future, Tony likely will be skittish of Sam. He won't exactly feel like asking him over for dinner.

So, what's to learn here? Well, when you're wrong, you're wrong! There's no defending it.

Thus, you should say up front, *"I blew it, no excuses!"* And don't negate that admission with a grimace or demeanor of displeasure that belies your sincerity.

Nor should you act like you want to give the matter short shrift. That's a common tact. It also contradicts earnestness.

At times, such admissions are agonizing. You want to justify your actions and convince yourself that you're not to blame. You might do that with flimsy reasoning, but it's unlikely that anyone else will buy it. So why compound the error?

In contrast, an outright admission of mistake could gain immediate respect, as well as understanding and compassion. And it eliminates the downsides mentioned above.

And keep in mind, humbleness is a likeable quality. Strange as it seems, putting yourself down, most times, doesn't really lower you in the eyes of another.

For example, say that Sam, the erring gentleman in our skit, says to Tony: *"Gee, I sure did a dumb thing in not rechecking that total. I could kick myself in the rear."* To that, Tony, no doubt, would say something like, *"Ah, forget it, Sam, I've done the same darn thing a zillion times."*

And, being humble can even be charismatic. Try it, call yourself a dummy, and you'll be amazed how persons will rally to your side.

But anyway, a tendency to be defensive is difficult to overcome. It must have its roots in childhood. But it can be done.

You do it, by bombarding yourself with the sheer irrationality and fruitlessness (not to mention disrespect garnered) of not admitting the hard truth. In other words, you really force yourself to face facts and exercise common sense.

Thus, try that if you have this problem. As they say in Spanish: *¡Vale la pena!* (It's worth it!)

Here and now, vow to admit goofs and offer no excuses.

How to Improve Your Relationships, Dramatically

Soften Negatives

They can become partial MakeFeelGoods!

*O*h, what a tiptoe task it can be to deal with distasteful or touchy things in relationships. The following are ways to sugarcoat them:

Firing or terminating someone: Under some circumstances, the jolt of this dreadful news can be tempered somewhat. You can do this, by using the you-orientated method. You try to make the termination appear best or better for the affected person. Here's a skit to illustrate:

Wally's supervisor, Carl, has to let him go. Wally just can't do his job:

> Carl: *"Wally, I've been studying you and this job, and I don't think it's best for your particular talents. You deserve something better than this. This job puts too much pressure on you. With your mechanical skills, I think you could do a lot better at something else. So, Wally, for your sake as well as the company's, I think it's best that you look for a better job."*

Thus, Carl's approach makes Wally think that Carl is interested in helping him. Carl places the emphasis on what's best for Wally, not the company. That's the beauty of this technique.

Ending a special relationship: This is another tough situation. It comes up usually in a romantic setting. For whatever reasons, one partner decides that she or he has had enough of the other. And, of course, telling the blunt truth would hurt too much. So, using the mentioned technique, you try to numb the pain. Here's how it works:

Patricia wants to break up with Larry. They have been going together for two years. More and more she feels that she just can't take his self-absorbed ways.

Patricia: *"Larry, I just don't think I'm the right person for you. You deserve someone more compatible with your likes and dislikes. I wish I were. I respect you so much. I just know that someone out there would be better for you. I want the best for you, Larry. And I know that I'm not it. For this reason, I want to end things."*

That approach does deaden somewhat the pain. Contrast that with how hurt and bitter Larry would be if Patricia had said the usual: *"Larry, I just can't take you anymore..."*

That's convincing, isn't it? The you-orientated method is a decent and considerate way to deliver a difficult message. It sure helps.

Take the blame: Do so even if you don't deserve it. This precept parallels a tad the one mentioned in the "You be the dummy" advice. To understand it, let's return to the skit where Sam, the vice president of the investment club, has botched an expense report. He made a $10,000 boo-boo.

Tony, the president, who discovered the slip, could make

Sam feel better in this way:

Tony: *"Gee, Sam, I'm so sorry I didn't tell you how critical that expense total was going to be this month. Had I told you that, I'm sure you would have caught this $10,000 discrepancy. Please forgive me for not emphasizing how important that report is."*

Sam (Grinning): *"No, kidding? It's off $10,000? Wow! Forget it, Tony."*

Sam's comment says it all, doesn't it? What a switch. Now he's forgiving Tony instead of the other way around.

And the bottom line is that despite Sam's blunder, Tony has made Sam feel better about himself. That's the goal here.

Now let's look a bit closer at this kind of a situation. Let's say that you're partially, not wholly, to blame for a boo-boo. Still shoulder complete blame. Here's an example:

Dad has a dental appointment at Daughter's dental office tomorrow. He calls her the day before to ask her to bring the large scrapbook he had given her. He wants to show it to someone.

So the next day Dad arrives at Daughter's office. Daughter tells him that she has the book for him. He then has his teeth cleaned and spends an hour or so in the process.

But alas, upon leaving he forgets all about the book. And so does Daughter. (In other words, both goof).

That night Dad regretfully remembers. He calls Daughter.

Now here are two approaches he can take:

(1) *"Doggoned, Daughter, you forgot to give me the scrapbook! Did you get busy or something?"*; or

(2) *"Gees, Daughter, what a lunkhead I am. I completely forgot to ask you for the scrapbook when I left."*

So, it's obvious which of those two Dad should take. But it's a sad commentary that most people use number one.

And it's a MakeFeelBad! So, take heed!

Now here's a way of taking undeserved blame. It can prevent hard feelings and preserve a relationship:

Ceilia to Melinda: *"Let's meet at the library tomorrow afternoon at 4:00. OK?"*

Melinda: *"Great, see ya then. That way we'll have time to finish the project before class [it starts at 6:00]."*

The next day Melinda arrives at the library promptly at *4:00.* But Ceilia is not there. She doesn't show up until about *4:55.* By then it's "iffy" if they'll have enough time to finish their project.

Ceilia: *"Gosh, Melinda, you're early. How long have you been here?"*

Melinda: *"I've been here since 4:00. I thought that's what you said."*

Ceilia: *"Oh, no! I said 5:00. You agreed."*

Now, Melinda can respond in one of two ways:

(1) *"Just a minute, Ceilia, you clearly said 4:00. Come on now;"* or

(2) *"Oh, my golly! I'm so sorry, I misunderstood you. I'd better get the wax out my ears. Let's get to work."*

Knee-jerk like, Melinda opts for number one, just like most of us would do. The chagrin of having to wait an hour blinds her as to how harmful words like that can be.

She doesn't realize that such a response sets a negative stage for the job she and Ceilia have to do together. Yes, Melinda's ire keeps her from seeing the wisdom of response two. That is, by taking undeserved blame she can limit the consequences of Ceilia's goof to the time lost and nothing more. She can prevent an adverse impact on their relationship and what they can accomplish together.

But in the heat of frustration, those things don't weigh in with Melinda. So, she gives Ceilia a piece of her mind. And their chances of working well together go out the window. That's too bad.

But in Melinda's defense, it really asks a lot to shift blame to yourself when you don't deserve it. This is especially true when you're miffed, upset. You have to forgo comeuppance. That's tough!

You have to make a hasty analysis: *"Will what I want to say help or hurt?"*

Usually the answer is simple: Blaming hurts. Taking blame helps.

Cushioning-prefatory comment: Now switching focus a bit here, here's an excellent way for you to ease the sting of telling someone, *"You blew it."*

> *"William, if you have about eight hours or so and about three legal pads handy, I could tell you about all my goofs in this business. But unfortunately, this time we have to talk about one of yours."*

Such prefatory words by William's boss help ease the shock of what William knows is now coming. Just knowing that his boss makes mistakes too, makes William feel a tad better. *"Hey, maybe I'm not all that bad. And I sure have a good boss."*

Criticizing or critiquing a work: Here's the inviolate rule: good, bad, and good again. Now that sounds somewhat cryptic. But it's simple, short, and can make an oceanic difference in how well your input is accepted.

You divide your analysis into three discussions: (1) good points; (2) bad points; and (3) good points again.

Here's how: If circumstances permit, at the outset, spend considerable time discussing everything you like about the work. And watch for eyes to sparkle and a grin to spread. That's what the good-news part does.

It also cushions the bad that's coming. Plus, you can make the bad stuff more palatable if you preface it. That is, if the work even marginally warrants kudos, say something like this: *"Boy, you've done such a good job, it's hard to find something wrong. But if this were a course in critiquing, that is, I just have to find something wrong or flunk, I would say... [et cetera]."*

After you wind up the negative with suggestions for remedying it, again accent the positive by returning to pluses. Repeat in different words what you previously said that you liked.

Then, if it's not too implausible, offer praise for the overall work. This is crucial.

Following this procedure helps the medicine go down. And most important, it handles with care the feelings of the other person. Pride is on the line.

In contrast, when criticism is inconsiderately, carelessly given, it can blast to smithereens a person's hopes, dignity, and confidence.

And this is done far too often. So, take heed and get the above technique down pat.

The touchy question: It's tough to ask something that has an accusatory tone. In essence, it's a *"Did you do it?"* or *"Are you guilty of so and so?"* query. The mere asking, can insult or offend. So, how do you do it in the least offensive way?

Well, try the technique used by the experts on television. Some are masters at asking sensitive questions.

The thrust is to put the accusation in the mouths of others. In other words, the questioner is not the accuser. Someone else is. Here's how it usually goes:

Questioner: *"Mr. Jones, what do you say to those who say you're cheating the poor?"*

Mr. Jones: *"I say it's not true. I've never taken a dime from the poor."*

Questioner: *"But what's your response to those who say they have canceled checks and witnesses?"*

Mr. Jones: *"I say, baloney!"*

As you can see, the method makes it unreasonable for the questioned person to turn on the questioner for something the questioner did not say or do. That's the key.

The technique works well under the scrutiny of the public (no one wants to appear unfair) and with reasonable persons. But with others, especially, when no one else is within an earshot, watch out. You still might get clobbered.

But anyway, when you don't want to hurt a relationship by asking a thorny question, that method is worth a try.

The touchy person: Almost everyone has had a close relationship with a testy person. This is someone difficult to get along with. At times it seems that such persons love to argue, be disagreeable. They seldom can accept what other persons say at face value without nitpicking something.

Nevertheless, with a little forethought and discretion, many times you can disarm such a person. How? Well, listen up.

The following is a how-not-to. It leads with the chin: Dad, a retired person, usually mows Son's lawn every Monday. It's now late Monday afternoon. From his office Son calls Dad:

Son: *"Dad, did you mow the lawn at the house today?"*

Dad: *"Gees, how about giving me a chance to do it, Son. You know I've got other things to do besides your stuff!"*

In contrast, here's a how-to. It defuses, defangs the nitpicker:

Son: *"Dad, I know you have a bundle to do, and it's difficult for you, but have you found time yet to mow my lawn?"*

Dad: *"Not yet, Son. I'll get to it later."*

Here are more examples:

Daughter on telephone: *"Dad, would you read me Mom's letter?"*

Dad: *"Right now? Geez, give me a break! I don't have time now."*

The better way:

Daughter: *"Dad when you can find time, would you call back and read me Mom's letter?"*

Dad: *"Will do."*

Thus, the method entails anticipating possible objections to or quarrels with what you intend to say. In advance, you cover all bases and leave the cantankerous one absolutely nothing to pick on. It works!

So try it and practice it. It sure can make it easier for you to get along with a touchy person. The technique can be a godsend when that person is someone vital in your life.

Suggestions and instructions: As we all have learned the hard way, making and giving these, sometimes can be a walking-on-eggs situation. This is especially true in a close relationship.

Things like jealousy, rebellion, and resentment easily can rear their ugly heads. But even if such feelings are not a problem, tact is always in order.

One of the best ways to make a suggestion or give an instruction is to do it indirectly. That is, do it by asking for the other person's opinion. Here's an example: Mom wants Son to take typing in school next fall. Rather than directly telling him to register for the class this spring, here's how she handles it:

Mom: *"Son, what do you think of you taking typing next fall? This will help you in your other classes. You'll be able to type all your homework. And it will also help you get a job when you graduate."*

Son: *"Yeah, I see what you mean. Boy, that would give me a leg up in my other school work. Yes, great idea, Mom."*

In this way, Son is less likely to feel like it's an order thrust upon him. Rather, he will feel like he's part of the decision-making process.

That is one key to making suggestions or orders palatable. Have persons participate. That way they are less likely to oppose what they help evolve.

Moreover, it's one more way that tact can serve your close bonds well. Try it.

Hopefully, all the above shows you skillful ways to handle distasteful or delicate matters that come up in your bonds with others.

You need to master these skills!

Taking It Out On Someone

What a MakeFeelBad!

*T*his conduct is so inexcusable! Yet just about everyone commits this wrong now and then. And not many things do more harm to relationships. Here are some common ways to commit this offense:

Killing the messenger

For umpteen reasons doing this is a no-no, not the least of which is that it doesn't make sense. To blame the person who brings you information for creating it, is off the wall. That's the nub of the wrong.

In childhood, we learned that this reaction is unjust. We heard about the king who beheaded the messenger for bringing him news that his army had lost a battle.

So, we know it's wrong and illogical. But we all have an unrealistic, human expectation: *"Tell me what I want to hear, not what I don't."*

That's the thinking you must battle. If you don't keep it at bay, you punish those who bring you important but unpleasant tidings.

And unfortunately, it's so facile to come down on a bearer of grim news. Sometimes, it's done without realization. It can be subtle, but nonetheless harmful.

Now here's a common way it's usually done:

Wendy and Ryan are married and work for the same company. She is telling Ryan what their boss, Sandra, said to her at a meeting the day before.

Wendy: *"Sandra took me aside and told me that I should talk to you. She said that I have to get you to stop berating other employees. She said that they're complaining about you."*

Ryan (face turning red and with raised voice): *"What the hell is that nonsense? That's a lie! You know damn well, Wendy, I don't berate anyone. Why, you work right with me. You know better than that!"*

As you can see, Ryan, is talking to his wife as if she were Sandra. Yes, illogically and unjustly, he is turning Wendy into the person making or believing the charge. He's making her pay dearly for simply having passed information on to him.

But at least Ryan is limiting his venom to words. Some persons throw things, break things, slam doors, et cetera.

Nevertheless, whether it's words or actions, it's misdirected. And it's destructive to a relationship. After Ryan's tirade, his wife feels brutalized, penalized by his words.

Clobbering the handy

Oh, what a common sin this one is! Someone has a miserable day at work, comes home, and takes it out on who's ever handy. Too often this is an unlucky spouse or a child. How unjust!

And it's behavior equally irrational as is killing-the-messenger. It involves the same type of misdirected ventilation and anger. And it smacks of a bully's tactic. The actor picks on the innocent and defenseless.

Blaming the blameless

Now here's still another nightmarish behavior that butchers relationships.

The following skit illustrates it well.

Bob Smith, an attorney, receives a call at his office from a deputy-clerk of a court:

> Clerk: *"Mr. Smith, I'm calling to tell you that your motion for a new trial has been dismissed. This is because no one from your office appeared at the hearing on the motion this morning. I will put a copy of the judge's order in the mail. Please call if you have any questions. Thank you, Sir. Bye."*

Agape, and furious, Bob slams the phone down so forcefully that he breaks its cradle. He turns to Carla, his secretary, and kicks her desk like it's a football. The jolt knocks her keyboard to the floor.

The blow leaves a notable dent in the desk. All the other employees nearby look up, shocked. In panic, they scatter out of the room.

> Bob: *"Carla, why in the hell didn't you remind me of the Jones motion for this morning? Damn it to hell, you cost Jones a new trial!"*
> Carla: *"Sir, you didn't tell me about it. I didn't know."*
> Bob (still enraged): *"Well, you should have made it your business to know. That's your job!"*

Obviously, Bob goofed, and he's trying to make it Carla's fault. He doesn't want to admit to himself that he blew it. And, even if he had told Carla about the hearing, for something so critical, he should not have depended on her alone.

So, anyway you look at it, the buck stops with Bob. And whatever the state of his relationship with Carla was, well, it deteriorates considerably. His behavior is just another example how taking it out on someone can do just that.

So, if you tend to punish persons handy when things don't go your way, how do you get yourself to stop? Well, you do it by blasting yourself with blunt logic. You tell yourself over and over how unfair, illogical it is to take it out on an innocent somebody. You think about how adversely that can affect your tie with such a person.

Rub your nose in that inescapable-dire result. Enough said.

"You were right!"
Do You Say These Words Often Enough?

*I*f you do, you're an exception. Most people do not, and they miss an opportunity to make someone feel good.

This topic was covered somewhat in the *Praise* MakeFeelGood. But because it's such a critical factor in relationships, let's take a closer look.

With most people, getting them to say the words, *"You were right"* is like pulling their teeth. That's because if the words eventually do come out, they usually have to be yanked.

And guess who has to do the yanking! Right you are, it's the person who deserves to hear those words.

But having to yank them out defuses them. They lose significance. They might as well not be said.

Now here's a skit that illustrates this problem:

Carla, an astute business person, engages Thomas, a close friend, who is an experienced real estate expert. She wants him to show her some homes.

After a week of looking, they find one to Carla's liking. But the home needs substantial repairs.

Carla: *"Thomas, these repairs change the ball game. Also, the sellers have moved out, and they want to rid themselves of the house. Bottom line: I think these people will take $6,000 less. I think that's what I should offer them."*

Thomas: *"Carla, do you want some sound advice? I've been in this field for 25 years. And I think I know sellers and the market. If you offer them that, you'll make them mad. You'll lose this deal. Offer them only $2,000 less. Again, if you go lower than that, you won't get this house."*

Carla (after a long pause): *"Well, Thomas, I'm willing to take that chance. My gut tells me I have a good chance of getting it for $6,000 less. I'd like you to submit my counteroffer for that amount."*

Thomas: *"OK, but I hope you won't be too disappointed when this deal bombs out."*

So, Thomas faxes the counteroffer. Three hours later the sellers' agent calls and tells him that the sellers have accepted. Thomas calls Carla:

Thomas (as if he's reporting something ordinary and expected): *"Carla, they accepted your offer. The closing will be on the 14th. The sellers' agent wanted to make it the 20th. I said no."*

He goes on and on about sundry details. But does he directly or indirectly say crucial words to her like: *"How right you were?"* No way!

And Carla says nothing to remind him. That's not her way. She thinks Carl, on his own, should admit that he was wrong. His failure to do this offends her.

So, for persons like Thomas, why is saying those little words, *"You were right!,"* such a big deal? What's the problem?

One word is the answer, ego. Persons so plagued by their egos feel that saying those words amounts to an admission. It's an agonizing one that they don't want to make even to themselves.

So, what is the admission? Well, it's the fact that some persons might be smarter than they. And they delude themselves that they can avoid this reality by ignoring evidence of it.

Of course, this is fantasy. And it's destructive fantasy.

That's what it is, because it hurts bonds. The ones who do not get credit for good judgment are bound to be miffed.

So, when someone deserves to be told, *"You were right,"* **say so,** right off the bat. Don't do it fifteen sentences down the line or have to be prodded to do it.

Cast aside ego!

"*We*"

is a teeny-weeny word!

$\mathcal{B}$ut it's such a key MakeFeelGood. So, in a close relationship, try to invoke this tiny word's spirit. Yes, invoke the feeling that the two of you are a team. You do things together. You share together.

And this goes as far as sharing credit even if it's not wholly logical or justified. *"What?,"* you ask, skeptically.

Yes, you should do that. It can be most constructive. Here's an example:

Nellie and Edgar are brother and sister. They're close. Edgar is writing a thesis for a college course. He's been at it for a month or so. And now and then, Nellie, two years ahead of him in school, helps him with ideas.

On the Friday before the Wednesday the paper is due, Edgar is pouring over the task. He is frustrated with his effort's blatant mediocrity.

Then, his guardian angel, Nellie, bails him out. She makes his day by giving him a humdinger of an idea.

Edgar latches onto it like it's a life preserver. He embodies it pronto. What a difference! The paper now brims with excellence.

Two weeks later he gets his grade, a shiny A, no less. And, Nellie, of course, is delighted:

Nellie: *"Oh, Edgar, I'm just so thankful that on that final Friday we got that idea for the new approach. We finally saw the light. We are quite a team."* [Though it was Nellie's idea, she uses that tiny, potent word]

Edgar (grinning ear to ear): *"Amen, sweet Sister."*

And his love and respect for her edges even higher, if that's possible.

So add that teeny-weeny word to the list of potent-little ones. The skit shows how much using it instead of "I" can do for a bond.

Nellie shows that she is not concerned with ego. Getting credit for what really was her inspiration, doesn't mean beans to her. All that matters is her brother's welfare and feelings.

That's how you must feel. This is the core of the point here:

> *The relationship has to be more important to you than self-aggrandizement. And when that feeling comes from the heart, a key relationship is bound to thrive.*

This One's For You!

$\mathcal{Y}$es, this final MakeFeelGood is for you. This is because at this point you just have to feel good about what you have learned here. You now know that if you practice this book's recommendations, your relationships will prosper. This will happen because with important-to-you people, *you will:*

- *Show interest* in them.
- *Compliment* them.
- *Listen* and *respond* to them.
- *Not interrupt* them unnecessarily.
- *Praise* them.
- *Not use "I"* too much.
- *Build their self-worth.*
- *Not talk down* to them.
- *Thank them* adequately, when appropriate.
- *Tell them white lies* when appropriate.
- *Show them courtesy and consideration.*
- *Not be defensive* with them.

- *Soften negatives* for them.
- *Not take it out* on them.
- *Tell them* they were right when they were.
- *Have a "we" spirit* with them.

But you also now know that making these practices habitual won't be easy. It will be difficult to keep them from falling by the wayside, preys of out-of-sight, out-of-mind attrition. That's what happens to so many things we learn.

A good example is what has happened to much of what we learned during our school years. Immediately after learning many things, we had them well ensconced in our minds. Then, shortly after final examinations, wham, it was adiós. They left us!

The point is, there's only one way to reap the benefits of what this book teaches. You must come up with some system to constantly remind yourself of what you have learned.

For openers, don't do with this book what most of us usually do with one after we finish it. We put it on a shelf or give it away.

Do not do that! Instead, keep this book handy for almost constant reference. Keep it on hand until you have instilled the above-sixteen measures as second nature.

Use it like you would a manual to operate some mechanism. You keep it near the machine for quick reference.

Well, the machine here is your brain. This book is a behavioral manual for it. So it has to be handy, readily accessible at all times.

That means keeping it in a purse, briefcase, gym-bag,

or what-have-you. Just keep it at hand.

Thus, by whatever means, you must keep reviewing, almost daily, the sixteen precepts. Perhaps, you should even tape record the above short-list summary. Listen over and over.

Also, you regularly have to critique yourself. *"How did I do today? Let's see, let me get the book out. How did the way I handled that problem with Betty comport with what the book says about things like that?"*

Hopefully, you now see how critical it is that you *don't give this book away.* Or that you don't relegate it to book heaven, out of sight or mind on a shelf on your favorite bookcase. Again, you have to *refer to it often.*

That's the key! Do that and implement religiously the above magical sixteen, and wow! Your bonds with others will become so sound, so rewarding for both sides.

But in fairness, you should know that a not-so-rewarding aspect exists to using these skills. Some persons will regard you as a gull. They will consider your "goodness" as "stupidity" and try to take advantage of you. *So be on guard!*

And when you stop such persons in their tracks, don't be surprised if they take umbrage: *"Why, how dare you stop letting me kick you in the shins, you mean person!"*

But let's hope that few such persons will be in the mix for you. In any case, hold your ground. And chalk that drawback up to the seemingly worn-out — but at times still most apt — cliche: "There's a price of a ticket to every show." This one is worth the price.

And finally, if there is a bottom-line principle in this

book that you should latch onto tenaciously and never, never let go of, it's this:

> *Constantly strive to leave the important-to-you persons in your life feeling good or better about themselves after their contacts with you.*

This book has shown you methods to help you do that. If you use them, your relationships are bound to improve, dramatically. They could flourish. And if they do, you will reap much love, respect, success, and happiness.

Guaranteed!

Frank F. Loomis III, J.D.

*A*ttorney Loomis is a semi-retired trial and appellate lawyer, as well as an ex-corporate executive. His legal experience runs the gamut from murder trials to appeals as high as to The United States Supreme Court. In the business world, he has spent some twenty-nine years dealing with people while running three corporations.

He is an alumnus of Northwestern University, and the University of Notre Dame where he received his doctorate.

But his wisdom about interrelating with people is not based on academic considerations. Rather, it comes from years of dealing with people in business, legal, and family worlds.

Thus, he doesn't write and teach like he's in front of a blackboard lecturing about complex theories. That's the approach that many writers take in this area. Often their backgrounds are limited to classrooms or consultation rooms. As a result, their works are technical mumbo jumbo that bores readers.

In contrast, Attorney Loomis writes in a way that you don't have to be an academic to understand. He talks plainly about close relationships and how to improve them. The things he suggests are practical, easy to grasp, and apply.

And he is eminently qualified to help people in this area. This is because his expertise is the best type of all, practical experience in dealing with thousands of people. He has learned what he teaches the hard way, by trial and error.

His special knowledge stems from his relations with the hundreds of employees and co-workers that he has trained. And it also evolves from his dealings with clients, jurors, judges, attorneys, witnesses, legislators, business associates and the seven children that he has raised.

Thus, his vast experience in real world settings has given him a grass-roots-practical know-how about close relationships. His teachings are not abstract theories learned from textbooks. Rather, they are down-to-earth-practical suggestions applicable to everyday situations. They can help anyone, regardless of educational level.

So, that's Attorney Loomis' background. And you can see why it makes him uniquely qualified in a most practical way, to write about this critically important subject. And persons who follow his counsel can take a gigantic step toward improving their relationships with the persons most important to them.

Index

Order Form

Fax Orders: (210) 495-3073

Telephone Orders: (210) 495-2937 Please have your Discover, Visa, or MasterCard ready.

On-line: glennb@flash.net

Mail Orders: Glenn Publishing
17906 Winter Hill
San Antonio, TX 78258

Please send me _____ copies at $17.95 each of
How to Improve Your Relationships, Dramatically,
ISBN: 0-9672089-0-4.
Contact the publisher for discount on more than 5 copies.

Name: _____

Address: _____

City:_____ St:_____Zip: _____

Telephone: (_____) _____

Shipping:
$4.00 for the first book and $2.00 for each additional book.

Payment:
☐ Check Enclosed or
☐ Credit card: ☐ Visa ☐ MasterCard ☐ Discover

Name on Card: _____

Credit Card No: _____

Expiration Date: _____/_____